contents

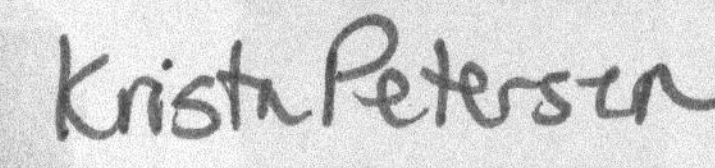

//not beyond reach

How to Share Jesus with the Young, the Deconstructed, and the Non-Religious

Foreword by Chip Ingram

Aaron Pierce

Published by Living on the Edge

ISBN 978-1-60593-501-0

Printed in the United States of America

//not beyond reach

How to Share Jesus with the Young, the Deconstructed, and the Non-Religious

acknowledgments

This book is a result of the collective effort and wisdom of so many incredible people.

To my wife, Jen, the rock of our family. Your strength and compassion are beautiful, and I am so grateful for you. To my kids: Asher, Selah, Hudson, and Wesley. I pray every day that you will love Jesus and follow hard after Him.

To my parents, David and Jodi, who are the heart and soul of our mission. Your authenticity and unwavering commitment to following Jesus has inspired so many people around the world, including me. The principles in this book are a reflection of the incredible lives that you have lived.

To my brother, Ben, who I have had the joy of running this race with since the beginning. You have always challenged and pushed me.

To Tristan Hanson and Katie Lounsbury, who put hours of work into this project behind the scenes.

To the entire Steiger family. You inspire me. This book is a reflection of your stories.

To Chip Ingram. Your investment and generosity toward me is more than I possibly could have asked for. Thank you for believing in me!

To everyone at the Living on the Edge team (especially Kitty Allen, Jerry McCauley, Heather Sellars, Anita Palmer, Thom Hoyman, Cara Iverson, Vicki Fulgham, Chris Tiegreen, Mike Olson, and Maraya Pearson). Thank you for your hours of tireless work.

foreword

I remember the day I first met Aaron Pierce. He attended a pastors-appreciation gathering that I was speaking at about ten years ago, and we connected after the event. I could just sense a very special calling on his life and the Steiger ministry.

He gave me a copy of his dad's book, *Rock Priest,* and as I read it, I sensed a strong prompting from God that there was something more for Aaron and me to unpack together. It was clear that not only was this young man passionate about reaching young unbelievers for the Lord, but he was actually doing it!

As a father and grandfather, I am passionate about reaching the next generation with the truth of God's Word. And I'm very aware that at this stage of my life, I am less of an expert on how best to connect with the global youth culture. As Aaron and I got to know each other better, my respect for him and Steiger's approach to reaching young people all over the world grew exponentially. I found myself not only intrigued by their global impact but also eager to help get Aaron's teaching on this topic into the hands of more believers. I'm thrilled that Living on the Edge is partnering with Aaron to bring this message to life.

It's no secret that our culture continues to grow more and more hostile to Christian values. And our tried-and-true methods of reaching the lost are less and less effective, especially as young people in the millennial and Gen Z age groups become more skeptical and less trusting of institutions in general and the Church specifically.

I have had countless conversations across America with believing parents who are puzzled and heartbroken when their children—after they've finished high school, started a job, or returned home from college—say that they are skeptical of biblical morals and no longer interested in pursuing a relationship with Jesus. In even more extreme cases, some have rejected traditional views of gender and sexuality. This is after growing up in a Christian home, possibly attending a Christian school, and being active in their church youth ministry.

The stakes have never been higher for Christian parents, grandparents, and pastors to be equipped to navigate these challenging situations with truth and love. The spiritual lives of our beloved family members hang in the balance.

Unfortunately, our instinct as believers is to isolate ourselves from these divisive issues. We recoil in fear, not knowing how to move forward. But I believe that God is calling us now more than ever to not back away but instead engage and move into these relationships with compassion, concern, truth, and hope.

In reality, our children have never been more anxious, depressed, hopeless, and confused than they are today. The gospel is and has always been the answer, but we must rethink and revise how we communicate it by life and word.

In the pages that follow, Aaron takes you on a journey and unpacks, step by step, how you can reach the next generation for their good and God's glory. He clearly outlines the difference between showing compassion to the lost and affirming or accepting their behavior.

At first, you may find what you read to be challenging for your worldview. Just as Jesus rocked some of the religious and accepted traditions of His day, this book will challenge how some of us have unintentionally built walls between the gospel and our next generation loved ones. But I can confidently say that Aaron's approach is not only biblical but also very effective. It is a time-tested and proven concept.

The Steiger ministry, which Aaron leads, is reaching the global youth culture in one hundred major cities worldwide. I've met with his staff, taught in their training center in Germany, listened to their stories, and witnessed God's power reaching young people who would never walk into a church. Aaron himself has spent his entire life living out this relational way of reaching the lost all over the world, and it is more achievable than you may think.

As a pastor for almost forty years, I'll be teaming with Aaron by adding insights and specific application for parents, grandparents, and pastors to help build bridges to those they love. I trust that God will use this book to equip you and fill you with courage to be the winsome messenger of His truth to a generation that is *not beyond reach.*

Chip Ingram
CEO and Teaching Pastor, Living on the Edge

introduction

My brother and I were raised by missionary parents in Amsterdam, a historic city full of beautiful cathedrals and churches that were virtually empty on Sundays. The majority of Dutch people were non-religious. God was a relic of the past, irrelevant to the present. Yet my folks had a passion to share Jesus Christ with the young generation, so they went where they were: in clubs and bars late at night.

My parents and their teams would befriend the people in the clubs and bars and, whenever possible, share the gospel. Then they'd write down the names of everyone they met and go out into the forest and pray all night, asking God to draw each person to Him.

At the height of the 1980s punk-rock movement, the ministry expanded to include a band that grew in popularity in Amsterdam and beyond. Many of the young people who responded to my father and his bandmates' message of God's love attended a "rock-and-roll" Bible study held on a big red barge on the river behind the city's central train station. Hundreds would come to "Steiger," which is what the ministry came to be called. (It's a Dutch word meaning pier or dock.) Eventually, the study grew into a church, and Steiger (and the band) had success all over Europe, including in Poland and the Soviet Union.

Because Dad brought us along, my brother and I experienced first-hand how following Jesus was not just a religious tradition on Sunday but a real and powerful transformation of lives. Today, if there ever was a generation that needs to experience that power, it's the post-Christian global youth culture that has only grown in influence and scope. Millions of secularized young people are walking away from Christianity. These deconstructors and the non-religious have rejected the concept of "truth" and believe that the only thing that matters is doing what feels good and being true to oneself.

But they are not beyond reach.

The Church, however, needs to understand those young people's culture and go to where they are, as my parents did. We can't wait for them to come to us.

In this book, we're going to learn the language, values, and assumptions of the global youth culture. We're going to discover ways to meet them where they are. We're going to practice authentic friendships and build trust by listening and genuinely trying to understand how they see the world and what they believe, without compromising our own beliefs and principles.

After that, we're going to learn the next step, which is to open up spiritual conversations, affirming what we can and gently challenging their worldviews. Whatever their deep-seated needs and passions are, we'll look for ways to steer the conversation toward the biblical story of creation, humanity's fall, the death and resurrection of Jesus, and the redemption available through a personal relationship with Him.

Finally, we're going to address some of the divisive issues that inevitably come up in conversations with people who do not see the world through a biblical lens—especially in subjects related to politics, sexuality, and science. These conversations actually create great opportunities to reframe the gospel in ways people can clearly understand. But we need to be prepared by learning how to navigate tough topics.

Over the years, I have seen countless lives changed through someone boldly and creatively sharing biblical truth with people and introducing them to the person of Jesus. I've seen people accept Jesus in nightclubs, on university campuses, on city streets, in drug-saturated environments, at gay-pride events, and in almost any context imaginable. I know the process works—not as a method or technique, but as a means of pursuing the people God loves and fulfilling the mission He has called us to.

That's His heartbeat, and it needs to be ours, too. The next generation is crying out for meaning and purpose, and followers of Jesus can point them to it.

But we have to know how. Reaching a post-Christian culture may feel overwhelming and intimidating. But with the Holy Spirit, everything is possible! My prayer is that this book will equip and empower you to live out God's truth and share it in a culture that often questions whether truth even exists. If you are willing, God will lead you into the kinds of relationships that connect with people's hearts and transform lives. Let's get started!

1// The Rise of the Post-Christian Culture

Sydney was wearing a rainbow-colored shirt with the word RESIST *and an equal sign on it. She and some friends were outside the state capitol in Sacramento, demonstrating at a large pro-choice rally. With both sides of the abortion debate facing off and heckling one another, the mood was tense.*

Filipe and a small group mingled in the crowd, asking God to guide them to people open to talking. Without identifying themselves as Christians, they struck up a conversation with Sydney and those around her.

At first, Sydney and the others talked only about their political agenda, openly identifying as nonbinary and hostile to traditional morality. Filipe and his friends listened intently. When they did ask a few questions, Sydney surprised them with some vulnerable answers—about the pain and anger behind the banners and the rainbow clothing.

Filipe empathized with the hurt the young people had experienced. He said that he had learned the way to heal life's pains was spiritual, not political. The others nodded. Then he said, "And no matter how distant God may seem, He is not indifferent to our suffering. Jesus's death on the cross was proof of that."

Sydney and her friends were shocked. "What? You're a Christian? How can you believe that Bible stuff?"

Filipe was smiling now. He asked if they had ever read the Bible (they hadn't) and if they knew it was actually a love story. He challenged them to read it themselves and offered to help them understand what it said, no strings attached. After Sydney and her friends exchanged contact information with Filipe, they let him pray over them.

Sydney and her companions are among millions of young people in the United States today who are so far outside the sphere of Christian influence—and so hostile to the Church—that they might seem unreachable. But they aren't. Deep down, everyone is wounded, longing for relationships and belonging, and open to truth.

How can the Church learn to communicate the gospel to a new, non-religious generation?

Navigating the Post-Christian Cultural Shift

Over the past few decades, America has been undergoing a profound cultural shift. For much of U.S. history, most people viewed Christianity positively, whether or not they believed what it taught. The Bible was considered a moral guide, even if the majority of Americans didn't read it. Its general ethics undergirded civic life. The Church was the center of life in most American towns and cities, and church attendance was the norm. Church leaders—pastors, priests, evangelists, seminary professors—were still respected. In fact, a prominent one, such as Billy Graham, prayed at the inauguration of every U.S. president.

We now live in a post-Christian society. Increasing numbers of people have walked away from the Church: prodigals who want nothing to do with Judeo-Christian morality, and "deconstructors," who once had a faith but have torn it apart and discarded it. And there are many who are simply non-religious, completely uninterested in anything to do with religion.

//Over the past few decades, America has been undergoing a profound cultural shift.

Recent research suggests that the fastest-growing religious group in the United States is the religiously unaffiliated—the "nones." The entire category constituted 29 percent of American adults in 2021, up from 19 percent in 2011. The shift is most pronounced among millennials (born 1981 through 1996) and Gen Zs (born 1997 through 2012). According to a new study, 38 percent of millennials were nones in 2016; that jumped to 44 percent in 2022. Gen Z was made up of 39 percent nones in 2016; now the share of this generation who identify as religious nones is 48.5 percent.[1]

Our culture is radically changing. The study makes the point that "Generation Z is the least religious generation in American history."[2] Not only that, but

> every day in the United States, thousands of members of the Silent and Boomer generation are dying off. Every day in the United States, thousands of members of Generation Z are celebrating their 18th birthday and becoming official adults. That simple fact is changing American religion and society in ways that we can only begin to understand now.[3]

Unsurprisingly, attitudes in America toward Christianity are changing dramatically too.

A Believer/Unbeliever Spectrum

One way to represent how the modern Church is viewed is to visualize five categories on a spectrum.

On one end of the continuum are *committed* followers of Jesus. These are people who see themselves as strong or faithful Christians, attend church fairly frequently, and seek to align their lives with biblical truth.

Next to them would be people who have a *positive* view of the Church and may see the Bible as a moral guide and consider themselves Christian, even if they don't have a relationship with God or aren't very intentional in trying to live out their faith.

A little further beyond them are those who are *apathetic*: people who aren't consciously rejecting God but don't think about Him very often. Christianity makes little difference in their daily lives.

And at the far end of the spectrum would be the final two categories: people who have a *negative* view of the Church, and people who have a *hostile* view of it, like Sydney at the Sacramento protest. Some were raised in the Church and left it. Some see it as outdated or a symbol of repression and bigotry.

Of course, which of these categories the majority of Americans are in has drastically changed. In 1990, the percentages would have looked something like the chart that follows. Compare the numbers to those compiled in 2022.

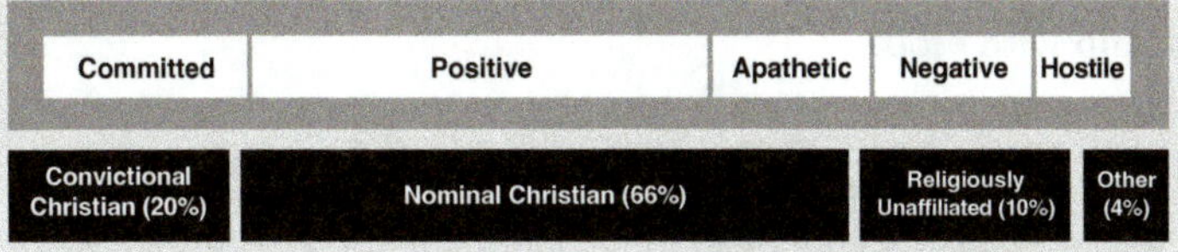

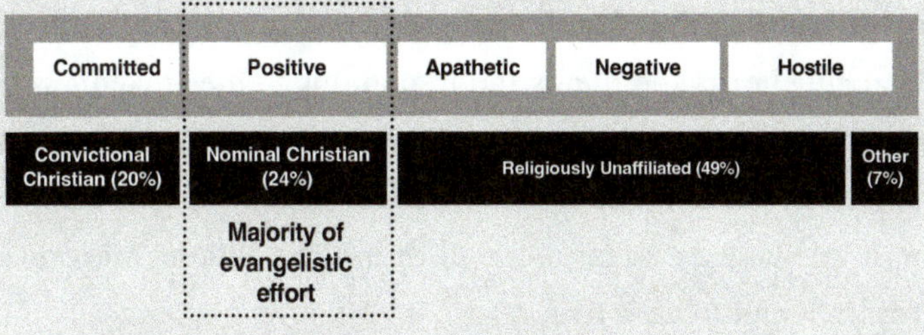

Redefining "Christian"

Another way to look at this shift is as a progression from one end of a continuum to the other: from convictional Christians to cultural Christians, "progressive" Christians, post-Christians, and, ultimately, non-Christians.

- **Convictional Christians:** people who actively follow Jesus, try to align their values and lifestyles with biblical truth, and live out their faith with conviction.

- **Cultural Christians:** people who may have a positive view of orthodox Christianity and consider themselves to be Christian, though it tends to be more of a social identity than a personal relationship with God.

- **Progressive Christians:** people who believe in God and identify as Christian but have let go of many of Christianity's core beliefs, such as the authority of the Bible. They shape their faith according to how they want to see reality.

- **Post-Christians:** people who are living out the natural consequences of progressive Christianity. Once Christianity has lost its connection with biblical authority and power, it is no longer effective in changing hearts and minds and responding to the brokenness and pain of life. This can show up as hostility for those who have been wounded by the Church or otherwise developed a negative perception of it. Many are so far removed from the Christian faith that it seems irrelevant to their lives.

- **Non-Christians:** people who may not know anything about Christianity, and if they do, they have chosen to ignore it or reject it. More and more young people in the United States fit into this category because they grew up in non-Christian homes, often due to their parents taking steps away from the Church and actively or passively rejecting it.

Examining Deconstruction

When I speak to audiences about the post-Christian shift, I often show videos of "deconstructors" on TikTok. *Faith deconstruction* is a popular phrase with a range of meanings, from simply reexamining faith to demolishing it.

One example of that extreme version of deconstruction is a young woman who went from being a devout Christian to an agnostic atheist. Here's how she describes her journey:[4]

> I loved being part of a church. I loved volunteering, serving on the worship team, and going on mission trips. But as I got older and experienced adult life and hardships, I witnessed the hypocrisy and politics that go on behind the scenes. I was disgusted and shocked at the corruption in the Church, the one place I thought I was safe.
>
> So I decided to take my relationship with God home, out of the Church, and make it a one-on-one journey with Him. I met people outside the Church who lived lifestyles that, I had been taught, would cause them to go to hell—people who followed other religions or no religion at all, who believed differently than I did and grew up in different ways. I had been raised to think these people were not capable of displaying real love because they weren't Christians. Yet they were some of the healthiest, most loving people I had ever known. So my faith started progressing, deconstructing things I'd been taught, questioning theologies I'd once taken as fact.
>
> I decided to dive deep into the Bible and my pursuit of God, hoping it would strengthen my faith. But the deeper I dove, the more questions that came up. I got a broader understanding of the Bible, its history, science, and my worldview in general. I realized I didn't even have enough reason to believe there was a God, much less the Christian God.

She went on to talk about how she cried out to God and begged Him to reveal Himself, even to punish her if she was wrong, but was met with silence. Little by little, she lost her faith and ended up being opposed to Christianity itself.

Sadly, this young woman's story is not uncommon.

The Church has often struggled to create an open environment where tough questions can be wrestled through within a Christian community. People's doubts are dismissed as lacking faith or immediately labeled as heretical and dangerous, with no room for conversation. Even though there are good answers to these tough questions, many people are left to deconstruct on their own or with other deconstructors online.

In the end, feeling wounded or at least not protected by the Church, many turn against it and live as though it doesn't exist. Others, like this young woman, become very vocal about their opposition.

Updating Old Evangelism Models

How has the Church been addressing this post-Christian shift? For the most part, we haven't. We lean into trying to reach the middle groups from the "Attitude and Affiliation Towards Christianity" chart: the cultural and progressive Christians. We've ignored the categories less like us on the far end of the chart: the post-Christians and the non-Christians.

Historically, the evangelical Church has used a "come and see," or "bring a friend," model of evangelism. It can be effective to a point, but it does not bridge the growing divide between our country's Christian and secular subcultures.

The truth is, though, that as resistant as many post-Christians and non-Christians seem, as far from God as their words and behavior might suggest, people are hurting and hungry. They are open, even when they don't appear to be. As followers of Jesus, we clearly need to respond. We can't wait for people to come to us; we have to go to them.

But how?

Missionaries in Our Own Cities

This is a huge paradigm shift for some Christians. Many in the Church are living under the illusion that we share the same culture with post-Christian and secular society. We don't. If we think we'll be able to communicate using the language we've always used, we're going to find that it is no longer understandable to the people we're trying to reach. We need to learn to share the gospel in ways they will understand.

//We can't wait for people to come to us; we have to go to them.

That means we need to become cross-cultural missionaries to our own people in our own cities. If you were called to be a missionary in a foreign country, you would need to physically go there, learn the language, become embedded in the culture, understand the worldview of the people there, recognize their felt needs, and contextualize the gospel in a way that would be meaningful to them. That's classic, cross-cultural missions.

Other than moving to another country, those things are exactly what we need to do in post-Christian American culture today. And we can't just send out a few specially chosen people to do the work. Each of us, every follower of Christ, needs to learn to see this as a calling and engage this culture from a missionary perspective.

That requires a radical reorientation.

We have to engage in ways people will understand. To do that, we need to understand *them*. And we need to adopt a missionary mindset.

Three Key Realities

To effectively communicate the gospel to a post-Christian culture, it's important to understand three key realities.

• **Secular people have become suspicious of religious institutions and are far less likely to attend a church event.** Trust in organized religion has plummeted over the past two decades. In 2001, 60 percent of people reported a high level of confidence in religious institutions.[5] Now it's only 31 percent.[6] In the eyes of many, the Church has lost credibility.

It isn't just the Church, by the way. People have lost trust in institutions in general—corporations, government agencies, anything that represents "the establishment." A first wave of mistrust undermined confidence in the 1960s and '70s, and we are now in a second wave of eroding confidence in institutions. The Church is unfortunately part of the package.

The implications are clear: If our primary way of engaging people is inviting them to a church event, then we're likely putting a stumbling block in the way. We need to start by building relationships.

• **Secular people today do not hold the same beliefs about truth, existence, morality, the authority of the Bible, and the nature of God that earlier generations did.** Try to imagine going to your nearest state university and asking an average secular student this typical evangelistic question: If you were to die today and God were to judge your life, would He let you into heaven?

You might get a blank stare, because that question makes all kinds of assumptions that an average young person may not hold to be true, God, judgment, and heaven among them.

Effective communication is all about knowing your audience's presuppositions and either challenging them or building on them. We'll talk more about that later, but to start with, it's crucial to recognize that our culture's assumptions have changed.

• **Secular people are often open to spirituality.** Though many people no longer hold to a biblical worldview, most are not absolute atheists. They believe in some form of spirituality, even if it's vague. That means they are at least open to discussion.

My ministry did a focus group with secular young people on the subject of spirituality. What they said was very illuminating. A twenty-three-year-old woman captured a very common sentiment about spirituality: "It's a feeling for me. Maybe it's not a being or a person, probably not, but I think that there are human experiences, like when you hold a newborn baby. I think there's energy, a force that lives."

That quote illustrates how people believe spirituality is good but that affiliation with a church or other religious organization is unnecessary.

That's why many people in our culture are attracted to meditation and Eastern religion: It's spirituality without authority and accountability, and it's personally adaptable. It gives people an opportunity for spiritual expression the way they want it.

The three key realities we've discussed here are important because if we're going to be good missionaries to our culture, they help us understand the context we're living in. They are core perceptions that are shaping our society.

The Influence of the Global Youth Culture

The post-Christian shift can be traced back to the eighteenth century, when the Enlightenment began to undermine assumptions about absolute truth and universal morality. But it has exploded into mainstream culture over the past few decades because of the emergence of what I call the global youth culture.[7]

We live in an era of unprecedented connectedness in which mass media, global economic networks, and the internet have eroded cultural boundaries. Because worldwide connections transcend borders and divisions, with online conversations now international in scope, young people are more similar than ever.

Youth the world over are influenced by the same voices, following the same social media influencers, playing the same video games, listening to the same music, and therefore sharing many of the same values. Much of what they share is superficial—fashion trends and musical tastes, for example—but they also share deeper values and perspectives, such as worldviews, lifestyles, and morality. Youth culture is truly global because young people all over the world are able to connect through it.

Four key influences play a huge role in shaping the global youth culture.

- **The entertainment industry.** This includes music, film, theater, and sports. What appears to be a mere pastime is actually a vehicle for shaping worldviews. Entertainment presents a way of looking at the world, including a moral framework. It has always communicated values—that's nothing new—but among youth, it is now doing so with a global audience.

- **Social media influencers.** Content producers on TikTok, YouTube, Instagram, and other social media platforms are connecting with audiences all over the world too. This is unfiltered communication—direct from the content creator to their audience—and the message is whatever they want it to be.

- **Video games.** The average twenty-one-year-old male has spent about ten thousand hours playing video games—the same amount of time estimated to master a fine art. The reach of the video game industry is bigger than that of Hollywood, and numerous young people are finding their identity and sense of accomplishment in online games that connect them with other players anywhere in the world.

- **Pornography.** In global youth culture, sexuality is simply a personal pursuit of pleasure and happiness, so pornography is considered neutral, with no adverse consequences. It is assumed to be harmless. It has become so common and pervasive that people talk openly about it without any sense of shame and with little awareness that it is rewiring their brains and distorting their views of love and relationships.

These four influences, unconstrained by any geographic or political boundaries, converge to shape worldviews of millions of young people. In fact, they have much more influence than politics, laws, and more traditional means of communication.

//Influencers with millions of followers are driving global culture.

Scottish writer and politician Andrew Fletcher said, "Let me make the songs of a nation, and I care not who makes its laws." Even in the seventeenth century, Fletcher recognized that the cultural influences of poets and philosophers are far more influential in society than those of politicians and judges. We're seeing that principle at work today. Influencers with millions of followers are writing the "songs of a nation"—or actually the world—and driving global culture.

There are three philosophical pillars supporting the worldview of the global youth culture.

• **Secularism.** This is not a new term, and most of us are familiar with it. It represents the compartmentalization of faith from social life. It doesn't necessarily mean people are atheists, just that faith is a private matter. You can believe whatever you want as long as you don't push your beliefs on other people. Secularism has affected the Church as well. Many young Christians believe it is wrong to evangelize because they have been influenced by the idea of secularism.[8] In a secular worldview, faith becomes detached from public life, which is theoretically supposed to remain neutral.

• **Relativism.** Secularism naturally leads to relativism. If beliefs are relative to each person and marginalized from public life, then there is no absolute truth or universal morality. Morals and values are preferences. We each have the ones we like, kind of like choosing a favorite flavor of ice cream. But one person's preferences don't apply to anyone else. All are equally valid.

- **Acceptance.** Open-mindedness and authenticity are highly valued. Each person should be accepting of everyone else's beliefs and choices, creating a culture of inclusion. The problem is that "inclusion" generally means including all people and ideas except those that are exclusive, which paradoxically makes this value of inclusion exclusive itself. This value used to be expressed as tolerance, but it's no longer enough just to tolerate other people's differences and the way they live; we must affirm them, a constant message in the global youth culture.

What's fascinating about these philosophical pillars is that they are all, in one way or another, twists on biblical truth. Post-Christian culture didn't invent itself out of nothing. It didn't invent itself at all; it has evolved over time to become a hot mess of foundational truths that have been distorted and adapted to fulfill the demands of a fallen world.

This creates some interesting paradoxes, such as activists commendably fighting for social justice (a biblical moral issue) while simultaneously arguing that morality is relative. Even secular relativists instinctually long for absolute truth.

I experienced this recently on a visit to a coffee shop. The barista had a pin on her shirt that read, "Be human-centered."

"That sounds interesting," I told her. "What does that mean?"

"Well, it means you treat other people like you want to be treated and consider other people's needs above your own."

"Wow, that's awesome," I said. "Where did those ideas come from?"

//There is still a point of connection with biblical truth for us to build on in our conversations.

A little confused by the question, she looked at me and pointed to the pin, as if that's where those values originated. She was literally quoting Scripture but had completely divorced herself from it. It was a great illustration of the post-Christian shift in which people cling to a biblical framework they no longer acknowledge or even recognize. That's tragic, but it's also an incredible opportunity. There is still a point of connection with biblical truth for us to build on in our conversations.

Global Youth Culture Beliefs

If we dig a little deeper and distill down to a summary of the global youth culture's beliefs—their general position on these four key components of a worldview—here's what it looks like.

- **Origin.** A secular worldview tends to combine naturalistic evolution with an Eastern religious "energy"—spirituality without accountability. Most secular, post-Christian people give scientific answers for how the earth and life came to be, but many still long for some kind of spiritual meaning. Eastern religion tends to be individualistic and low commitment, which fits the anti-institutional biases of secularism. The result is a scientific explanation for the origin of life, and an energy, or life-force, approach to understanding how it works.

- **Morality.** Morality is considered by most secular people to be a social construct, a purely human invention. At the same time, they believe social injustice must be fought with passion, creating an odd combination of relativism (in principle) and absolutism (in practice)—a philosophical denial of moral absolutes but a strong sense of obligation to establish justice.

- **Purpose.** There is no purpose other than to seek personal happiness and live life to the fullest. Within that, some people will identify a purpose of addressing injustice, saving the planet, treating others well, or living with integrity—a way of making the best of the life you have. But these values do not point to any big-picture, overarching purpose.

- **Destiny.** The most common answer secular people can give about if there's life after death is, in one form or another, "I don't know, and I try not to think about it." It's a scary question, and atheistic or agnostic answers aren't very satisfying, so most people try to avoid it altogether. Some will say they think about it at night when they can't go to sleep, and their response is often to distract themselves by pulling out their phone and scrolling through social media. The implications are just too big and terrifying to dwell on.

Secular Humanism, or the Religion of Self

If we had to identify a religion for the global youth culture, based on its worldview, it would have to be secular humanism: the religion of self. In secular humanism, God has been replaced and human beings have become central. There is no outside authority to tell us how to live. Meaning and purpose are therefore turned inward, so the key to happiness is found within. Just follow your dreams and don't let anyone tell you who you are or what you want. Resist all external claims to authority or absolutes. Above all, take care of yourself.

In the era of "my truth," all matters of identity, purpose, and morality are personally constructed. No one defines those things for individuals other than the individuals themselves. Everyone makes their own meaning.

If you're observant, you'll see this message everywhere—in songs, social media memes, conversations, advertisements, branding, and much more. Young people are not the only ones embracing this message, but it is the most common set of beliefs among the global youth culture.

For example, Jay Shetty (a very popular English podcaster, author, and life coach) shared on Instagram, "The rules are fake. Do what you want, listen to how you feel, and make decisions that honor your soul." That is secular humanism.

Or consider the poster I saw in a Starbucks. It was promoting the Born This Way Foundation and had the official Starbucks logo on it, but the centerpiece of the poster was a quote by the singer Lady Gaga: "Don't you ever let a soul in the world tell you that you can't be exactly who you are."[9] Again, that is secular humanism.

Sounds very appealing, doesn't it? Just believe in yourself and shut out any contrary voices. Authenticity is a matter of being true to your inner feelings and desires. Your entire purpose is self-actualization: becoming who you believe you ought to be. In this worldview, there is no other inherent purpose in the world to be discovered, and certainly none to have to conform to. The only purpose is the one you construct yourself.

The Heartbreaking Consequences

Not long ago, a non-Christian friend from high school posted on social media that his son, who is the same age as my oldest son, was diagnosed with brain cancer. I could hardly imagine the fear and pain he must have been experiencing. I scrolled down and read the comments on his post. People were sending him "positive thoughts," "healing vibes," and "much love." Although his friends' comments were compassionate and empathetic, there were no concrete words to support him, no encouraging truths shared.

In secular humanism, there is no transcendent hope. The consequences of this worldview, especially for our youth, is devastating. In a world in which a solitary individual, all by themselves, defines truth, that person inevitably ends up confused. In a culture that says to do whatever makes you feel good, the result usually is sexual brokenness and disgust. When everything is always about you, you wind up lonely. And when there's nothing to cling to other than yourself and whatever positive vibes you can muster up, you might experience anxiety, depression, and other mental health challenges.

Those are the logical consequences of the secular humanistic worldview. They are almost universally experienced in this generation.

As followers of Jesus, we have the ultimate answers to these things. Jesus brings truth to the confused, and healing and restoration to the broken. A relationship with the Creator is the ultimate relationship, and He promises peace beyond comprehension.

All the solutions to these crises, the devastating consequences of a religion of self, are found in Jesus. But sadly, tragically, even though we have the ultimate answers to the cry of this next generation, they are not looking to the Church for answers. So we can't wait for them to come to us; we have to go to them.

Broken Hearts Change the World

These people we need to help are our friends, children, and grandchildren. When we hear of the confusion, brokenness, isolation, anxiety, and depression of this generation, our response should be like Nehemiah's when he found out the people of Jerusalem were in trouble and that much of the city was still in ruins: "When I heard these things, I sat down and wept" (Nehemiah 1:4).

//These people we need to help are our friends, children, and grandchildren.

We aren't likely to do anything about the crisis of this generation until our hearts are broken. And the extent to which our hearts are broken is the extent to which we do something about it. This is a consistent biblical principle. Only when we allow our hearts to break will we make sacrifices, get uncomfortable, and lay aside our needs and desires in order to go after the lost.

Only God can change our hearts, but we can take the first step by repenting. We can confess, "Lord, my heart is cold and I don't care for people as much as I should. I'm sorry. Please forgive me and give me Your heart for the lost." That's a prayer God is happy to answer. His desire is to awaken us from our apathy and make our hearts sensitive.

If you sincerely pray like that, you'll begin to see the world through God's eyes and maybe see people's needs, fears, and pain for the first time. When He gives you a broken heart for people He loves, you'll find yourself willing to get uncomfortable and take risks—to take a step of faith, no matter how awkward it feels, because other people's needs have become greater in your eyes than your own comfort level.

Mission Impossible

If you've looked helplessly at post-Christian culture and felt overwhelmed by how impossible it would be to reach people immersed in it, you are not alone.

Nehemiah apparently had the same feeling when he heard about Jerusalem. His response? He prayed like never before. Biblical scholars estimate that he prayed and fasted for four months before he finally approached the king. "For some days I mourned and fasted and prayed before the God of heaven" (Nehemiah 1:4).

Though our mission may be impossible for us, we serve the God of the impossible. Nothing is impossible (or even difficult) for Him, and He will empower and equip His people to accomplish all He has called us to do. But it is not until we get on our knees in desperate prayer and cry out for Him to have mercy that we will see a breakthrough.

That's an invitation. As you pray desperately and take steps of faith—as God pursues broken, hurting people through you—He will do a work inside you and inside them to bridge gaps, soften hearts, and bring many into a relationship with Him. He will change the course of the next generation through the broken hearts, persistent prayers, and willing surrender of those who believe the youth we are aiming at are not beyond reach, for He is able to do the impossible.

A Word from Chip to Parents, Grandparents, and Pastors

I'd like you to pause for a minute and ponder how radically different this current generation thinks about life, God, truth, and relationships than most of us as parents, grandparents, and pastors do. Reflect on what it would be like to look at life in the way Aaron has just described in this chapter.

Empathy—really seeing life through the lens of this next generation—is the beginning of compassion. Do I agree with their viewpoint? Of course not, but the questions are, does it break my heart? Does it make me sad? Do I identify with how painful, difficult, and hopeless life can be for this generation?

Many of us as parents and grandparents and even pastors have responded with "I don't get it" or "That's crazy" or "How could anyone think like that?" or "What happened to them when they went away to school?" et cetera, et cetera. So often, our response is anger, feeling betrayed at times by our own children, feeling guilty that the world changed overnight and we missed it!

I encourage you to follow Nehemiah's example and what I've watched the Steiger ministry do: Cry out to God. As I spent time at the Steiger Missions School with their staff from all across the world, I heard young people weep, literally cry out in anguish, over the global youth in various countries, begging God to use them regardless of the cost.

If we're going to reach those far from God (many who grew up in our homes and used to attend our churches), it will begin with a deeply broken heart, and a desperate dependency on the Lord that will be accompanied by fasting, prayer, and the willingness to engage like never before.

I encourage you to read Nehemiah chapter 1 and use the cupbearer's prayer as a model for your own life. God loves the next generation deeply and is waiting for us to intercede for them and engage with them.

Let me give you a few questions to get your mind moving in a good direction as we continue this journey together:

1. Do I understand the culture the next generation is living in?
2. How healthy is my communication with my adult children? Do I know their hopes, dreams, and fears?
3. What challenges are my grandchildren facing, and how can I support them?

2// How to Develop Real Friendships with the Non-Religious

Lucy, a singer and actress, had romantic relationships with multiple people of differing gender expressions. So did most of her friends. She was immersed in the polyamory community, she said, because she had "so much love to give."

When her mother died of cancer, though, Lucy realized she was lonely. Her many connections ultimately were more superficial than authentic, and Lucy felt empty. When a coworker named Maria started to befriend her, Lucy was wary. But Maria seemed to show real concern. Lucy appreciated having someone to talk to who listened and demanded nothing in return. Even after Maria, a Steiger team member, mentioned she was a follower of Jesus, Lucy still wanted to continue a friendship with her.

Eventually, Lucy accepted an invitation to join some of Maria's friends for dinner and a Bible study. The warm acceptance she received opened her up to learning more about Jesus.

Truly becoming friends with people outside our Christian circles is a crucial means of sharing the gospel today. How can we reach the young, the deconstructed, and the non-religious in ways that are honest, intentional, and effective?

The Great Truth: We Want to Be Known and Loved

Humans are relational beings. It's hardwired into us. This reality is a reflection of the way God designed us. The very nature of God Himself is a relationship: For all eternity, the Father, the Son, and the Holy Spirit have been in community together.

So the great truth is that *everyone is looking for deep relational connection and belonging.* Everyone wants to be known and loved. People may put up barriers and come across as aggressive or disinterested, but you can bank on the fact that when you're talking with people, they are desperate for love and acceptance.

Yet people who do not have a relationship with Christ live in a culture that can leave them feeling empty and lonely. That's tragic. But it's also a huge opportunity, because the gospel offers what they are longing for and more.

The Loneliness Epidemic

Loneliness is at epidemic levels today. A recent study from Harvard University found that "61% of young people [ages 18–25] are reporting serious loneliness."[10] One of the reasons for this was the worldwide COVID-19 pandemic, but the study suggests that loneliness was an epidemic even before then.

We can identify several causes for the sense of isolation so many of today's young people feel. These include casual sex, delaying marriage, and interacting via technology.

• **Sex.** Society has largely rejected the biblical ethic of a sexual relationship shared between a man and woman in the context of marriage. Pornography and hookups are pervasive. Dating apps are connecting people with strangers not for the purposes of building long-term relationships but for chance sexual encounters.

A popular podcast examines big technology and its impact on our lives. Called *Land of the Giants*, its seventh season was focused on current dating culture. Here's what a guest (Allison Davis, a regular user of the dating app Tinder) said about relationships:[11]

> If I want sex or companionship, I can find it in these, like, little bites, enough to, like, sustain me and make me think, *Well I don't really need to try any harder than this because I sort of have my little snack platter. Why am I going to go for the entree, you know? Cooking a whole meal sounds too hard now.*

• **Delaying or skipping marriage and family.** When you're enjoying multiple sexual relationships and figuring out what you really want in a partner, why rush? People are ironically rejecting the bond and belonging they were made for in an effort to satisfy their desire for intimacy.

• **Technology and filtered reality.** People have never been more connected, yet they have never felt more alone. Online connections are often superficial and artificial.

What people experience now through social media platforms is a filtered reality. No one is presenting a genuine image of themselves.

Yes, people have always tried to present their best image. But now everyone is posting a curated and perfected version of themselves that far exceeds in-person image casting, so hardly anyone is connecting with authentic people.

• **Escapism and vicarious lives.** Rather than addressing their internal dark thoughts, many escape into the world of video games or endless scrolling on TikTok. Instead of facing the challenges and difficulties of life, more and more young people are responding to them by diving into an alternate reality and never processing those big thoughts in the context of relationships and a community of faith.

//When we befriend people, we are offering them a connection all of us long for.

In video games, you can live in a fantasy world, assume another identity, perform great feats, and win battles. You can more easily be the hero of a fake life than of your real one.

Related to escapism is the idea of living someone else's story. If people don't like their own lives, they can live vicariously through others, often a social media influencer.

Emma Chamberlain, for example, has about twelve million followers (and counting) on YouTube, and all she does is post videos of her doing daily life—usually nothing very interesting but just going through her day and commenting on everything she has to do. Her YouTube channel has been described as the Gen Z *Seinfeld*: a show about nothing. But young people love it because they connect with her and, at least for a moment, live her story rather than their own.

There's a song by a young woman on TikTok that perfectly captures what so many people in this culture are feeling. She sings of girls who are the life of the party and can take off their clothes and "nobody flinches" because they look like they're "made of honey and glass." After painting a picture of people who seem to have no struggles, she self-consciously reflects on her own image:

> And I wonder what it's like to be one of those girls
> To sit in the sun and look at the world and never think
> Wow, am I enough?[12]

Viewed by millions, the song's video clearly resonates. Living in an image-obsessed culture where life is lived online and everyone looks perfect feeds the overwhelming isolation. Experiencing someone else's life vicariously in an alternative reality helps relieve the systemic loneliness.

The Power of Friendship

Good old-fashioned friendship has great power to affect people's lives, especially in this lonely era. When we befriend people, we are offering them a connection all of us long for.

Friendship humanizes people. It's easy to be friends with people who are like us. We're called, though, to reach out to everyone—even those with whom we have little in common. Still more difficult to relate to are those whose values and lifestyles are way outside our comfort zones or possibly immoral.

But face-to-face interaction breaks down barriers. It's much harder to argue when you're sitting across from someone over a cup of coffee.

Friendship lets us demonstrate the gospel. Many secular people have false assumptions about who Jesus is and what His followers are like. They hold stereotypes and caricatures of Christians, often based on biased portrayals in the news and social media.

When we spend time with non-religious people, we can counter those misconceptions, especially by exhibiting self-denial and generosity, which go directly against secularism's religion of self.

There's a powerful scripture in Paul's letter to the Philippians that, if we can live it out, makes a memorable impression on non-religious people:

> Do nothing out of selfish ambition or vain conceit. Rather, in humility value others above yourselves, not looking to your own interests but each of you to the interests of the others. (Philippians 2:3–4)

Living that kind of life in front of secular people blows them away because it's radically countercultural. Secular humanism urges pursuing your own happiness. When people see someone lay aside their own happiness or self-fulfillment for the sake of others, it's intriguing to them. It opens up the opportunity to connect with people.

Friendship helps us understand other perspectives. Many Christians don't understand why secular people believe what they believe or know how to affirm the heart behind the convictions. That's one reason we have such a hard time bridging the cultural divide. Building friendships allows you to get to know others and eventually communicate the gospel in a way that connects with them.

Finally, friendship lets us earn the opportunity to speak truth. We live in an age of hypersensitivity. People are easily offended when their views are challenged—when they don't get the affirmation they think they are entitled to. When you build relational trust, you can speak into people's lives as a friend. You don't have to be talented, persuasive, charismatic, or an expert at apologetics; you can just be a good friend. Anyone can do that, and if you're intentional about engaging with the people God has put in your life, you'll have opportunities to speak truth.

//When you build relational trust, you can speak into people's lives as a friend.

The Lie of Affirmation

A great lie of our culture is that to be a good friend to someone, you have to support their lifestyle or worldview. According to secular doctrine, tolerance is not enough—we must affirm!

I experienced this firsthand at a district-mandated "inclusion and acceptance" conversation with other parents at the public school my kids attend. At the first meeting, several parents brought up a range of topics, including the dynamics of LGBTQ+ inclusion. One of the mothers made a statement that perfectly expressed what we're dealing with in our culture: "I think it's important to understand that tolerance is not enough. We must affirm."

The assumption is, to be friends with a person, we must accept whatever they think and do. Love equals affirmation.

Jesus beautifully demonstrated a contrary truth. He showed us that association and relationship with "sinners" is not synonymous with affirming their lifestyle. He freely associated with people who had been marginalized from society because of immoral lifestyles, yet He didn't hesitate to challenge them and tell them to "go and sin no more" (John 8:11, NKJV).

Jesus and Tribalism

One of the challenges of our day is the growth of tribalism, an "us versus them" mentality that has become a toxic trait of modern culture. Everyone is creating their own "tribe" of followers on social media platforms, and algorithms facilitate these virtual cliques. Any comment, question, or critical thought can provoke labels, and the public discourse gravitates toward straw-man arguments about the other side.

The human instinct toward an "us versus them" mentality isn't new. It's been present throughout history. One of the best examples in Jesus's time was the polarization between the Jews and Samaritans. Samaritans were descendants of intermarriage between Jews and Gentiles, and because of this "mixed blood," Jews hated them. And, of course, Samaritans resented the Jews' prejudices.

Jesus defied that tribalism in radical, countercultural ways. The best example is His conversation with a Samaritan woman He encountered at a well. His followers were shocked even though they had seen Him do many unconventional things.

The fact that she was a woman was one boundary He broke, as a man speaking alone with a woman in public was questionable. And talking alone with a woman who had a reputation for immorality (she had been married five times and was living with a man who was not her husband) defied every rule of that society.

But Jesus's love for people transcended cultural limits. As He said later in Luke 19:10, He "came to seek and to save the lost." He wasn't going to let society's rules keep Him from reaching someone who was lost.

If you read about the Samaritan woman in John 4, you'll notice that Jesus demonstrated remarkable love for her but never affirmed her lifestyle. He never told her, "Just be you," or, "Do whatever makes you happy." He was able to approach and befriend people of any background with great mercy and grace while also challenging their beliefs and behavior. That's our model for engaging this culture.

If we do that, we'll probably offend some religious people. Jesus often offended the religious people of His day because He spent so much time with "sinners."

When the tax collectors and sinners were gathering around Jesus to hear Him, the religious leaders muttered about how He welcomed those undesirable people and even ate with them (see Luke 15:1–2). Having a meal with someone in that culture was a sign of hospitality and friendship, an intimate gesture of acceptance. He never affirmed what those people did or believed, but He befriended them, and the religious people who were preoccupied with righteousness were constantly offended.

When you spend a lot of time with people on "the other side," you risk being labeled as one of them. That's a primary reason so many Christians are afraid to associate with people who are culturally, politically, or religiously at the other end of the spectrum. They're worried they might get lumped in with them—guilty by association. But if we're going to be like Jesus, it's a risk we have to take.

Relevance Versus Holiness

The Christian faith is full of paradoxes. In many ways, it's a set of tensions. One of those tensions is relevance versus holiness. Those two values look as though they're at opposite ends of the spectrum.

Relevance means being present with people in order to really know and understand them. It's about learning how other people see the world so we can communicate with them effectively. *Holiness*, on the other hand, is about being set apart—being different and distinct. One aligns us with people's hearts; the other distinguishes us from their lifestyles.

It's easy to err on either side of this tension. We can become so relevant that we start to look exactly like the world and adopt its perspectives, lifestyles, and morals in order to fit in. Our desire to connect can lead to those kinds of compromises. But we can also become so "holy" that we isolate ourselves from the world and become completely disconnected—with separate Christian schools, entertainment, businesses, everything. That extreme takes us out of the position to influence the world around us.

This is a false tension, of course. We can influence the world without compromising with it. Or, as is often said, we can be in the world and not of it. In order to transform our culture, we have to be both present in it and distinct from it. That's our calling.

Another lie is that in order to not be contaminated by the world, we must completely hide from it or isolate ourselves. Paul warned the

Corinthians about associating with Christians who were behaving hypocritically, but he followed up with a clarification:

> I wrote to you in my letter not to associate with sexually immoral people—not at all meaning the people of this world who are immoral, or the greedy and swindlers, or idolaters. In that case you would have to leave this world. (1 Corinthians 5:9–10)

Holiness did not imply disassociation. The truth is that we are called to go into the world and transform it by the power of the gospel.

Living in the World

I grew up in the Netherlands, and my brother and I had a friend we knew from our neighborhood. We left when we got older, but when I went back to Amsterdam years later, I decided to look up this friend. I went to his house, and he happened to be having a party.

There were a lot of people there, and many of them were smoking joints. They invited me to sit down and hang out with them. The "holiness" instinct in me could have said no and turned around to get away from any temptation or appearance of evil. The "relevance" side of me said, "Sure, okay." So I sat down with them.

//Another lie is that in order to not be contaminated by the world, we must completely hide from it or isolate ourselves.

They passed me a joint, which I just passed to the next person. I began having a conversation with them because I knew I wasn't going to be corrupted by them, just as Jesus wasn't compromised by the people He spent time with. I can hang out with non-Christian people and not be offended that they are acting like non-Christians. That opens up opportunities to connect and build friendships.

To live out the truth in this world, you'll need to be present with secular people but distinct in your lifestyle. So how do we live out this tension?

- **Be clear that you are a Jesus follower.**

This is not a bait-and-switch situation of hiding your identity as a Christian and then surprising people with it once you're "in," but also don't be obnoxious with your beliefs or come across as a "Jesus robot" who is oblivious to social cues and just keeps pushing Jesus. If you're truly friends with people, they should know you are a Christian since that is core to who you are. But that should come up naturally. It should flow out of the conversation.

- **Don't be surprised that non-Christians act and think in unbiblical ways.**

That's who they are. Many Christians are easily offended when someone acts a little rough or crude or makes a political comment they don't agree with. There's no need to freak out. That fits their worldviews, so we shouldn't expect anything else. We can still appreciate who people are even if they have a few rough edges.

- **Don't flaunt your moral convictions; instead, let people see your supernatural hope, love, joy, and peace.**

The goal is never to flaunt a morally superior lifestyle to secular people. While we strive to live a holy lifestyle, that is not what is going to change someone's heart. Morality is not even unique to Christianity; many religions and ideologies have behavioral standards that are comparable to ours.

What makes Christianity unique is that God does for us and through us what we could not do for ourselves. So, in your interactions with secular people, don't focus on your moral lifestyle, like the fact that you don't swear or get drunk. Instead, let people see the supernatural fruit of the Holy Spirit in your life.

If you receive a cancer diagnosis but still have joy and peace, if you have hope when everything around you is falling apart, if you love the unlovable or forgive someone who has hurt you, people notice. These responses are not natural; they are supernatural. The evidence of the work of the Holy Spirit in your life, not your morality, is what is attractive to the world. It points to something transcendent. When they see the fruit of the Spirit at work, especially in the midst of adversity, they wonder how it's possible.

This is why Peter told his readers to "always be prepared to give an answer to everyone who asks you to give the reason for the *hope* that you have" (1 Peter 3:15, emphasis added). Hope in the face of persecution leads people to wonder, *How is it possible to be filled with hope while going through such adversity?* The answer is Jesus and the empowering of the Holy Spirit.

There's a time and place for preaching moral truths. Letting God reveal His supernatural power at work within us will appeal to people of the world, who whether or not they realize it are seeking transcendence.

An Intentional Lifestyle

We've talked about the importance of building relationships with people who hold a secular worldview, but how do we actually do it? To start with, we need to adopt a missionary mindset—an intentional lifestyle that puts us in places and situations that allow us to develop friendships with the non-religious.

This is not a purely organic process. Missionaries don't just happen to show up in the country they serve. It's planned. We don't want to just stage our friendships because of an agenda, but we do want to be intentional about pursuing others, because God is intentionally pursuing them. That's our calling, and it requires an intentional lifestyle.

It's important to remember that we aren't befriending people solely with a goal of converting them; we're connecting with them to demonstrate God's heart for them, whether they ever make a decision for Christ or not. If we forget that, people start to become "targets" rather than friends.

Counting the Cost

One of the greatest addictions of our day is busyness. When we are involved in too many things, we have no room in our lives for building friendships. Relationships have a cost—time, energy, and

//We're connecting with them to demonstrate God's heart for them, whether they ever make a decision for Christ or not.

commitment—and that may require a change in our priorities and lifestyle.

The payoff, though, is deep friendship that builds and multiplies. Over time, you can build trust. When your friends see your lifestyle and character, they will be more receptive to you speaking into their lives.

Oikos and Relational Presence

The best way to start building relationships with non-religious people is by actively pursuing people in your *oikos,* a Greek word that means "household." It's more broadly interpreted as your sphere of influence. This is where you are most likely to be moved by a broken heart and be willing to count the cost.

If you are a parent (or grandparent) whose adult son or daughter has walked away from the Lord, or if you are a young adult whose brother or sister has deconstructed their faith, the best thing you can do is be a consistent, loving presence in their life. Pursue them. Meet them on their turf. Let them know that even though you may not agree with their choices or lifestyle, you love them and nothing will change that. Then pray and *never* give up. Their story is *not* over yet. Pray that God will bring other people or circumstances into to their life that will open their heart to Jesus. Be patient but always ready to respond when the Holy Spirit presents an opportunity to have a spiritual conversation and reintroduce them to Jesus.

Your oikos also extends beyond your family to neighbors and co-workers who need the transforming power of the gospel. You have more immediate opportunities to build connections with the people already around you than with someone you see only in passing or meet at an event somewhere.

The workplace is one of the greatest mission fields today. It puts us in front of secular people and creates opportunities for relationships. Ask God to highlight two or three people in your oikos who are far from Him who you can begin to intentionally pursue for a deeper relationship.

Expanding Your Sphere of Influence

You can also expand your oikos by being relationally present in secular places. Our culture has reduced our oikos and influence as people become more isolated. Neighbors don't engage like they used to, for many the workplace has been relocated to our homes, and families are geographically more separated than ever. Our spheres of influence are shrinking. A missionary mindset seeks to bridge those gaps and divisions and bring more people into our spheres.

We have many opportunities to do this. Remember, secular people are looking for community and a sense of belonging too. Go where people like to do things together. Organized sports, kids' activities, art museums, and book clubs are great places to connect with people naturally and build relationships.

So are causes, such as local politics, neighborhood groups, and volunteer committees. People who are involved in cause-oriented activities are displaying a desire to connect with something bigger than themselves. They believe the world is not as it ought to be—a solidly biblical perspective—and they want to make it better. Many conversations can stem from those perspectives, and those conversations can eventually turn to society's root problems and God's solutions for them.

Other public places—such as gyms, parks, bars, festivals, and fairs—are also conducive to connecting with others. You can develop authentic relationships by going there regularly and being engaged. Remember, these relationships and conversations don't just happen without showing some intentionality on your part. You are called to be a missionary in your city, and that is what a missionary does.

Going Where They Are

I led an outreach project a few years ago in New Zealand, a very secular, socially progressive country. Our group was in the capital, Wellington, and one day I saw a poster advertising an LGBTQ+ festival. I felt a deep conviction from the Lord that we should reach out because the gay community assumes that Christians are their enemies.

So I called up the organizers and introduced myself. I told the person on the phone that I was part of a Christian group and wanted to know if there was any way we could serve them at the festival. He was skeptical, but I assured him we would just be there to serve—to pick up garbage, serve water, and do whatever else they needed.

The organizers eventually gave us permission to set up a booth to serve water. When we arrived at the venue, we found out that we would be right between a porn-film booth and one where sex toys were sold.

There we were, the Jesus stall, right in the middle, giving out cups of water with these words written on them:

> *"Whoever drinks the water I give them will never thirst." —Jesus*

As it turned out, it was the hottest day of the year and we couldn't give away our water fast enough. Everywhere you looked, people were drinking water and reading their cups. We had hours of conversations with people who probably never would have intentionally talked to a Christian, but almost all of them were very positive.

A few weeks later, we were doing another outreach. A guy came up and mentioned that he had seen us at the festival. My wife and I started to talk with him. Over the next few weeks, we'd had dinner together and talked about Jesus. He had once thought of evangelical Christians as enemies, but he softened to the point of reading Scripture with us.

That kind of outreach may be way out of some people's comfort zones, but it isn't complicated. It just requires having a heart to reach people and being intentional about it.

A word of wisdom about this: Don't do it alone, especially in places that are spiritually dark or where you might experience strong temptations. For example, if you've had struggles with alcohol, don't go hang out at bars. Be clear about your motivation, and don't forget who is doing the influencing. Outreach is not an individual sport. It takes teamwork.

The cool thing about working as a team is that each person brings their own different gifts and strengths. There have been times when I haven't felt particularly strong or courageous, but if I know I'm doing outreach alongside someone else, I show up. Working with other people will keep you motivated, and it will also keep you accountable and safe so you are not being influenced by the scene but are influencers there instead.

Supernatural Favor: Person of Peace

As you seek opportunities to build friendships, ask the Holy Spirit to lead you to the right people and give you supernatural favor. Outreach is not just a human effort; it has to be Spirit led. Specifically, ask Him to lead you to people of peace. A person of peace is someone with whom God will give you supernatural favor and who will welcome you into their network of friends (Luke 10:6, for example). This person sometimes becomes a catalyst for others to be introduced to the gospel too.

// Ask the Holy Spirit to lead you to the right people and give you supernatural favor.

We see a great example of this in the gospel of Mark when Jesus encountered the tax collector Levi. "As he walked along, he saw Levi son of Alphaeus sitting at the tax collector's booth. 'Follow me,' Jesus told him, and Levi got up and followed him" (Mark 2:14). In the next scene, Levi has invited all his business associates—"sinners" in the eyes of the religious leaders—to a large meal to introduce them to Jesus. He was a person of peace.

People of peace may not have accepted Jesus as their Lord and Savior but are still open to the gospel message. That openness shows that God is already working in their lives. For example, Levi welcomed Jesus, opened his home, and invited all his friends over. The woman Jesus encountered at the well in Samaria ran back into the village to tell other people about Him. Many in that town became believers because the woman received Jesus into their community. This happened again and again with Jesus and the apostles in the Gospels and book of Acts because it is often how God works.

A person of peace is able to draw you into their world and help you make connections with their sphere of influence. This doesn't just happen, which is why it needs to be led by the Holy Spirit. He directs you to the right person at the right time—although you may not recognize that in the moment—to multiply your influence. But choosing to be available and intentionally go into places where non-religious people are happens first. Ask Him to lead you to people of peace, and doors will open for building deeper relationships.

Relax, Be Patient, and Don't Take Yourself Too Seriously

Once you're engaging with non-religious people where they are, it's important to remember some basic principles. First, *relax.* Be yourself and have fun. Sometimes being a little uptight comes with a missionary mindset, but remember that genuine friendship is not forced or orchestrated; it develops when people enjoy each other's company. Joy is contagious, so if you are finding enjoyment, others will too. Let yourself relax and enjoy the experience.

Second, *be patient.* Don't feel pressure to make something happen. You're not the one who does the work here; God is (1 Corinthians 3:6). Remember that the Spirit who led you there is the same Spirit who will work through you. But He doesn't rush things. Genuine relationships aren't instant. You'll need to take a long-term view of what God is doing.

Finally, *don't take yourself too seriously.* It's okay if reaching out feels awkward sometimes. It does for almost everyone. God is not relying on you to make everything go smoothly and keep everyone comfortable. Most people aren't worried about you; they're worried about themselves. So don't load yourself down with pressure.

Cyrena, one of the leaders of our Minneapolis team, is great at drawing people in with her joy. We were doing an outreach in the aftermath of the George Floyd tragedy right where it happened. I had been asking God to lead me to the people he needed me to interact with. I saw a couple there who looked kind of cool and edgy and I really wanted to talk to them, but I wasn't feeling very brave about it. So I told Cyrena, "I want to talk to those people."

She went bounding up to them and said, "Hey, you guys are cool. We should talk!" It wasn't complicated for her, as her joy is so contagious that people open right up to it. That's one of the benefits of working as a team, especially when you have people who help everyone just relax and have fun.

Harness the Power of Asking Questions and Listening

Listening is one of the most powerful expressions of love. Doing it is simple because you don't have to come up with answers and people like to talk about themselves—their needs, desires, hopes, and ideas and whatever else they feel like sharing.

I like to think of it as a three-step process:

1. Listen.
2. Ask questions.
3. Listen.

Not very complicated, right? But very profound. And by listening, I don't mean just hearing what they say. I mean really listening with a desire to understand. That's how you learn about people's real needs and desires, and it's what builds a sense of connection with them. The classic book on this is Dale Carnegie's *How to Win Friends and Influence People.*[13] It's filled with basic but powerful advice on how to create connection with people and develop friendships, and anyone can do it.

As you ask questions and listen, don't make assumptions. It's human nature to put people in boxes. We consider people's appearances, jobs, backgrounds or education and subconsciously assume that we know what they think or believe. It's important not to presume with people who have a secular, post-Christian worldview. They do not all think the same way, so we need to listen and try to understand.

//When you ask questions about how people feel and what they're going through, they very often will tell you.

Learn the real, raw stories people are telling you. Everyone is going through something, and if you're connecting and developing a relationship that goes any deeper than the filtered reality people tend to present of themselves, some of those problems and struggles are going to come out. When you ask questions about how people feel and what they're going through, they very often will tell you.

When Cyrena broke the ice with that couple at the site of the George Floyd incident, we all ended up talking for hours and we heard them share deep, vulnerable stories of brokenness. People are hungry for someone to listen to them, and if you build some trust with them, they will open up.

Really try to understand people's perspectives and how they came to believe what they believe. When someone says something you don't agree with, one of the easiest and most helpful responses is, "How did you come to believe that?" Then listen carefully to the answer.

Two things can happen when you understand why they believe what they do: You learn what the real issues are, what's really driving those surface opinions, and your understanding gives you a greater love, compassion, and empathy for them and therefore a deeper connection. Both are essential for building authentic relationships, and both will help you know how to communicate with others more effectively.

Remember, empathy is not the same as agreeing or affirming. Many people are afraid to listen and understand a view that is completely out of alignment with the Bible, because it might give the impression they accept it or agree with it. But listening and understanding does not mean you agree with whatever they say. Listening shows that you care—it has been said that being heard is practically the same thing as being loved.

Lastly, as you interact with people, find genuine ways to affirm the good that you see in them. They are created by God. They are unique. Look for ways to affirm that. Are they intelligent? Tell them! Do they have a special talent or skill? Compliment them on it. Do they have a kind, friendly personality? Tell them how much you appreciate it! By affirming these things, you are calling out ways that God has made them. Many people are starved for encouragement. When you generously speak life into them with your words, it's like water to a desert.

Call to Action!

- Do an honest review of how you are spending your time. What do you need to cut out in order to make more room for relationships with non-religious people in your life?
- Ask God to highlight…
  - **at least one person** in your *oikos* who is not following Jesus whom you will actively pursue for a deeper relationship.
  - **one place** (a hobby, cause, or location) where you will be relationally present in order to intentionally build new relationships with non-religious people. This is even more effective (and fun) if you commit to doing it with others.

Spend some time alone with God to seek His will and ask Him to reveal that one person and one place. Don't just pick someone or somewhere without praying about it. When He brings to light that person and place, write them down in a journal or somewhere visible in your house, like on a sticky note posted to your bathroom mirror.

Pray for the person and place daily, and then start adapting your lifestyle to pursue that person and be present in that place. That is what a missionary lifestyle looks like!

A Word from Chip to Parents, Grandparents, and Pastors

Fellow parents and grandparents, before you react to some of the things that you just read, let me ask you a question: Are we going to continue to focus on how terrible it is that almost 70 percent of our own children are leaving the faith after five years and are we going to blame the media, the culture, and the Church, or are we actually going to do something positive about it?

Let's face it: We who are older believers can be more than a little bit blind to how our tribalism—protecting our traditional values—pushes away the younger generation. Our confusion, hurt, and anger about the next generation's rejection of what we hold dear may be valid, but we must take the first step to breaking down the walls. It begins with us.

We need to be willing to have uncomfortable conversations. Start with open-ended, honest questions. Listen actively and make space for people to share why they disagree with you. Ask why they voted the way they did or how they feel about their friends who are LGBTQ+. Until we actually hear them and begin to understand where they're coming from, there's no real hope for two-way communication.

Imagine what would happen if you could change the way your children and grandchildren see you: not as outdated, over-the-hill, or completely out of touch. What if they could reflect on a conversation with you and think, *I can't believe I felt heard. They didn't try to convince me I was wrong or poke holes in my thinking. They didn't quote Bible verses to me. I know how differently we believe, but I was treated like an equal whom they value.*

This is an essential step to building a foundation with your children and grandchildren. If you don't start here, you may not ever hear what is going on in their hearts and lives. And more than that, they might not grasp how much you love them.

Please note: This chapter is about friendship, not compromising our values, biblical morality, or the truth in any way. Aaron is encouraging us to reestablish relationships and friendships in ways that are very uncomfortable for some of us. But for me personally, I'm far more uncomfortable watching us lose a whole generation and having my grandchildren feel condemned or that I don't understand their world than being in their corner and helping them with what they're facing. The principle of relational connection from the heart always precedes the transmission of truth into their lives.

3// How to Start Spiritual Conversations with the Non-Religious

My brother and I were in a coffee shop on the University of Minnesota campus hanging out with a dozen or so students. From their comments, they seemed typical of the global youth culture and the post-Christian society we live in. But we were engaged in a hot discussion about the idea of Truth—in the era of "my truth."

Was there such a thing as absolute truth, we asked them, or was all truth subjective and relative? If there were no transcendent code everyone needs to accept, how could we hold anyone to a moral standard? If truth were truly subjective, couldn't one person's evil be another person's good? Any judgment was simply an imposition of one person's truth on another, right?

Then Nico, a thoughtful man in his early twenties, spoke up. "What if we factor in the idea of love? I mean, if you're going out killing people because you think that's your truth, that's not a loving thing to do. So, I suppose love could be a foundation for which we can strive for the truth."

Nico's statement resonated with everyone. It opened all kinds of thoughts about the nature of love. I eventually was able to share that God is the source of all love and that Jesus represented the ultimate form of love because He sacrificed Himself for our sake.

As the evening drew to a close, people didn't want to leave. Some of them had started out skeptical. Many left saying their heads were spinning and they had a lot to think about. And this was cool: They didn't feel like strangers anymore. They had connected with everyone around that coffeehouse table.

My head was spinning too over how hungry today's youth culture is to have deep spiritual conversations. How do we break through the surface of indifference and reach the heart of longing? What is the best way to engage people in spiritual conversations?

Spiritual Versus Gospel Conversations

The key to communicating the gospel in a post-Christian culture is first to learn how to engage in effective spiritual conversations. Although secular people have become increasingly suspicious of religious institutions and don't share the same assumptions as previous generations, they are still open to spirituality. They might immediately put up their defenses with a mention of Christianity, but talking about what's important in life and how to fix the problems of this world is something they value. They may even venture into the deep, existential crises they are experiencing—the big, scary thoughts that keep them awake at night.

What is the difference between a spiritual conversation and sharing the gospel? A gospel conversation focuses on the biblical narrative of creation, the fall, and redemption that is centered on the life, death, and resurrection of Jesus. A spiritual conversation, on the other hand, is presuppositional. It addresses the underlying assumptions that the gospel message is built on and serves as a bridge to the gospel.

To put it another way, the first is the story itself. The second goes after the problems, needs, and longings that make the story relevant.

The key to effective communication, then, is knowing our audience's assumptions. Christians often fail to realize that when they share the gospel, they are drawing on assumptions that secular people may not understand or believe, so they don't connect with the message. We need to know when we're communicating with people that we are either challenging their assumptions or building on them.

//The key to effective communication is knowing our audience's assumptions.

Consider, for example, the classic evangelistic approach known as the Four Spiritual Laws. The first law is that God loves us and has a wonderful plan for our lives. Second, we have all sinned and our sin separates us from God. Third, Jesus is God's only provision for our sin; through Him, we can know and experience God's love and plan for our lives. And, fourth, we must individually receive Jesus as Savior and Lord so we can know and experience God's love and plan for our lives.

All of that is true. It's solidly biblical. But the approach does make a number of critical assumptions, most notably that a relational God exists and that there is a moral framework and transcendent purpose for our lives. Those ideas are built into this model, yet post-Christian culture is highly skeptical of them. Non-religious people are predisposed to rejecting the whole premise. We have to do more to lay a foundation for them to grasp it.

The purpose of a spiritual conversation is, therefore, to set the foundations for the message of the Cross; remove the intellectual, emotional, and cultural barriers that obscure the Cross; and move from the secular to the spiritual.

A Conversation Model

I classify conversations into three types.

- **Friendship conversation.** The purpose of a friendship conversation is to build a deeper relational connection and earn trust to share the truth. It's how we get to know people and they get to know us.

- **Spiritual conversation.** The purpose of a spiritual conversation is to explore assumptions, cultivate openness to spiritual truth, and set the stage for presenting the gospel. It addresses many of the concerns on people's hearts about life, relationships, values, meaning, and purpose.

- **Gospel conversation.** The purpose of a gospel conversation (which we'll explore more in the next chapter) is to share the message of Jesus and the Cross in a way that feels relevant to the person you're speaking to. It introduces (or reintroduces) them to Jesus and gives them an opportunity to say yes to Him.

In a society characterized by a cultural Christianity well established in previous generations, it could be appropriate to go straight from friendship to gospel conversations. That's no longer the case. Today, we need to contextualize the gospel. When we engage in spiritual conversations, we need to present the assumptions that are foundational for the gospel.

God's Sovereignty

Some Christians, however, do not accept the idea of a middle step. Focused on God's sovereignty and wanting to appear unashamed of the gospel, they believe it's their job to proclaim the "simple" gospel of Jesus Christ and that it's God's job to open people's hearts to receiving it. How the audience responds is not their responsibility.

Our dependence on God's power is absolutely true and right. We should never be ashamed of the message and always trust God to make it fruitful. But choosing between an effective approach and God's sovereignty is a false dichotomy. We can do both. As the late pastor and author Timothy Keller once tweeted, we don't need to "pit dependence on the Spirit against efforts to be understood. They can go together."[14]

We need God's power, we need Him to speak, and we need Him to open people's hearts. We also need to be wise, culturally aware, and sensitive to His leading as He works through us to do that. Both God's part and our part are essential.

A spiritual conversation is not about compromising or watering down the message; it's about clarity. We all try to communicate in ways we think people will understand. But how we put our thoughts into words is based on our assumptions about our listeners. And the listener is bringing his or her own assumptions into the conversation too.

We should seek to be understood in a relevant way so we can build a bridge from friendship to the gospel. And a key part of that bridge is having conversations about spiritual issues before we get to the gospel itself.

No Ideal Timeline

It's important to note that the friendship-spiritual-gospel conversation model is a helpful framework but isn't always perfectly linear. Conversations tend to blend together, bounce back and forth, and blur categorization.

Sometimes you'll get into a gospel conversation and be talking about Jesus and the Bible's claims of truth and then realize something is standing in the way. You need to deal with an underlying assumption that seems to be an obstacle, so you step back into a spiritual conversation, maybe to challenge the person about their worldview or a moral contradiction.

Other times you may strike a nerve and hit on a very personal issue, and the person reacts very emotionally and puts their defenses up, so you need to go back to friendship conversations to spend some more time building trust so you can speak into their life later.

Sometimes you'll be developing a relationship with someone and having a spiritual conversation and you realize it opens up into a gospel conversation that you might not have thought they were ready for. This can go in all kinds of directions. There is no formula.

Nor is there any ideal timeline. This whole process from friendship to spirituality to the gospel can take place within one conversation on an airplane with a stranger or occur in many conversations over a long period of time.

//Our friendship should not be conditional on them accepting our message.

But if the gospel is rejected or they are not ready to make a decision, that doesn't mean the friendship has to end. The process often takes time, and it's important that we stay committed to walking with people. Our friendship should not be conditional on them accepting our message.

Blinded Minds

A spiritual conversation is not just an intellectual conversation or an exercise in apologetics. It is bigger than just changing a worldview or reorienting how a person thinks. At its core, it's spiritual. It requires the supernatural work of the Holy Spirit to be effective.

This is clearly stated in one of Paul's letters to the Corinthians: "The god of this age has blinded the minds of unbelievers" (2 Corinthians 4:4). Spiritual blindness keeps people from seeing the truth. We are dealing with a generation that has been deceived and spiritually blinded. No matter how often you point at a wall, a blind person is not going to be able to see it.

Logic may be involved in our discussions, but this is not primarily about logic. When you're talking with secular, post-Christian people, no matter how often you point to the gospel, they aren't going to be able to see it unless the Holy Spirit opens their spiritual eyes.

That's why persuasive arguments, cool programs, and powerful presentations are never enough. Again, there are no formulas for this. The issue we face is having to overcome the spiritual blindness of a generation, so we must recognize that and prioritize prayer and dependence on God.

As we engage in conversation, we should be asking the Holy Spirit for supernatural discernment so we can understand the real issues. We are listening not just with our natural ears but with spiritual insight, discernment beyond our natural understanding. *What lie is this person believing? What is the core issue or assumption that is distorting their understanding? What idols are they clinging to? What felt needs are driving them?*

These are not questions we can answer with our own intellectual acumen, as sharp as it may be. We need the Holy Spirit to illuminate what is really going on so we can get to the heart of the issue. As we're told in 1 Corinthians 2:14,

> The person without the Spirit does not accept the things that come from the Spirit of God but considers them foolishness, and cannot understand them because they are discerned only through the Spirit.

That's the dynamic at work in all our spiritual and gospel conversations. We need spiritual discernment. Everything depends on the Holy Spirit showing up in the midst of the conversation.

Discernment from the Holy Spirit

The need for discernment really hit home for me once when we were doing outreach in Minneapolis. It was a warm summer day at a local lake, and we had music, games on the lawn, some barbecue, and many people who showed up. I was asking the Lord to lead me to someone and give me one good conversation with them.

I saw a couple on a rented scooter who had stopped right in front of our spot to see what we were doing. *That's them,* I thought. I waited a minute and then went up to them and invited them to join us. I felt as though the Holy Spirit was giving me some inside information about the young woman, like maybe she felt invisible and needed to be seen. I knew nothing about her, but I asked, "Hey, are you a singer?"

"I am a singer!" she said.

"You should go up onstage and sing. Come on!"

And she did! We rallied our whole crew to watch her as she played and sang some songs. She was just beaming. When she finished, she came off the stage and we talked for a long time. She and her boyfriend hung out with us and were open to learning more from the Bible. Later that evening, the young woman prayed to receive Jesus.

That wouldn't have happened if God hadn't given me discernment about her. It wasn't some weird, exceptional thing. We serve a supernatural God who pursues His children and wants to give us supernatural discernment to reach them. What we need to do in response is be sensitive to God's leading.

I know my own human efforts aren't good enough; yours aren't either. We need something beyond our own resources to soften people's hearts, open our eyes to what's going on in their lives, and open their eyes to truth. Only God can do that. We always need to be wise about our communication and depend on the Holy Spirit.

Pitfalls to Avoid

There are pitfalls we need to avoid as we have these spiritual conversations. If we aren't careful, the exchanges can go in an unhelpful direction and get stuck in one of three boxes: personal, religious, and political.

It's human nature to put people and ideas in boxes. The problem is that this subconscious categorizing can cause us to speak reflexively when certain cues trigger us. The same thing happens with the person you're talking with. They have their own boxes and triggers, limiting what they are willing to talk about and how they perceive our spiritual conversations. If we're going to have fruitful spiritual conversations, we'll need to specifically and intentionally recognize and avoid the following three boxes.

• **The Personal Box.** Many people today, including Christians, believe faith is a purely private matter that should not be discussed publicly. Believe whatever you want as long as you don't push those beliefs on other people. And "pushing" can mean simply talking about it. As a result, many people are hesitant to engage in discussions about spirituality. They put it in their "personal" box.

Your goal in this case is to challenge that kind of mindset by connecting spiritual conversations with everyday reality and implications. What people believe about big, spiritual issues shapes their lives.

With tact and sensitivity, you can bring those beliefs into an open discussion without coming across as inappropriately "personal."

• **The Religious Box.** In a post-Christian society, most people have had some engagement with the Church, either personally as they grew up or through the culture at large. Unfortunately, many have developed misconceptions about the Church and religion or have had direct, negative experiences. They equate all churches with hypocrisy, corruption, and control. The goal of a spiritual conversation is to explore the major questions of life without evoking the religious baggage that will distort their view of Jesus.

In many respects, this is a matter of language. I spent my teenage years in New Zealand, which has all kinds of regional slang. When I came to the United States, I had to adapt my language so that I could communicate effectively. It's similar with our "Christianese." Learn to notice when you use it, and don't let it become a barrier. Adapt to secular culture and learn its language so you can more effectively communicate.

• **The Political Box.** Some Americans associate the Church with a political party. They assume that when you talk about Jesus, you're also pushing an ideology they believe is oppressive and bigoted.

In chapter 5, we'll talk more about how to avoid that problem, but it's important to recognize the problem up front. Jesus should never be tied to a political perspective. We need to focus on core spiritual truths and avoid secondary issues that create barriers to connection.

Everything Is Spiritual

Almost everything we do and talk about has spiritual inferences. As followers of Jesus in a post-Christian culture, we need to tune in to that reality and become skilled at drawing spiritual associations out of everyday conversations.

> **//Your goal is to move prayerfully from secular topics to spiritual ones.**

As you engage in relationships with secular people, your goal is to move prayerfully from secular topics to spiritual ones. You want to get beyond the superficial in order to share deep, real, raw thoughts and feelings with one another. The best way to do this is not by making statements but by asking questions and then teasing out the implications. The good news is that there are many ways to go about this process and many topics that can lead to spiritual issues and relational depth.

Here is a list of categories of discussion and some key questions that help drive the conversation deeper.

SPIRITUAL TOPICS:

Family and Friendship

- What is the most important thing in life?
- Why are our closest relationships often the most complicated?
- Why are conflict, hurt, and disappointment so universal in relationships?
- Is there someone who will never let you down?

Purpose and Passion

- How can we find our purpose in life? Why do so many people struggle to find their purpose?
- Is purpose necessary to be happy? What makes life worth living?
- Is there more to life than just survival and the procreation of our species?
- Is there a transcendent purpose for all humans? If so, what is it and what is the source of that purpose?

Work

- Do you like your job? Why or why not?
- If you didn't need the money, what would you do for work?
- Do you think there is a difference between a job or career and a calling? What is a calling? Do you know someone whose vocation is truly a calling?

Happiness and Satisfaction

- What makes you happy?
- Why is happiness so elusive? Why is satisfaction so fleeting?
- Do you think it's possible to be 100 percent content in life? Why or why not?

Pain and Suffering

- How do you cope with pain and suffering?
- Why are there so many problems in the world? Can we fix ourselves?
- What gives you hope?

Morality and Justice

- What causes are you passionate about?
- Who gets to decide what is right and wrong?

- Are there universal human rights? Where do they come from?
- Why deny yourself for the sake of others?

Identity

- How do you define yourself?
- What is the core of your identity?
- What parts of your identity can't be taken away from you by circumstances?

Love

- What is love?
- Do you believe you can find that one person who will "complete" you?
- What is the ultimate expression of love?

Beauty

- Is there a song or film that moves you to tears?
- What is it about a sunset, piece of art, or newborn baby that inspires a sense of awe?
- Why does beauty feel transcendent, bigger than life? Why do we feel as though we need it?

Many of these questions get to the heart of what it means to be human. Almost everyone thinks about these things, but not many people talk about them. You can ask probing questions about life's purpose and what people are passionate about. Probe about identity, what dynamics shape relationships, and where our value as human beings comes from. The possibilities are endless.

Remember the motivation for having these conversations: to develop authentic friendships that give us the ability to ask harder questions and go deeper. At this bridge stage between friendship and the message of the Cross, the goal is to understand and eventually challenge underlying assumptions, to get people to think about why they believe what they believe, and hopefully for them to begin to see the incoherence and inconsistencies of a secular worldview but without putting them on the spot.

That's why questions are so much better than statements. Asking someone a question about the value of human life is much more fruitful than declaring which side you're on in the debate over pro-choice versus pro-life. It may point to the same issue, but it's framed in a way that doesn't squash your friend's thinking process. You want people to feel encouraged to wrestle with their beliefs. And in the course of those conversations, people become much more open to your thoughts on the matter.

Out of Your Everyday Life

Our team in Houston was out doing a prayer walk on Cinco de Mayo. Through a series of conversations with people they met, they were led to an artsy, secretive rave club that no one could get to without having some inside information. They had to go through a back door, up a staircase, across an empty room to another back door, and up another set of stairs before finally entering.

The club was dark and the walls were covered with graffiti. It was loud and packed with young people. One of the guys on our team was a suburban middle-aged dad named Roger, who felt very out of place. The team decided to split up and spread out to talk to more people.

Molly, a young woman who had been perched inside a hoop that hung from the ceiling, came up to Roger and Allison. "You look like cool people. What do you do? Not for work—just tell me what you're really good at!" She was genuinely interested.

Roger wasn't sure what he was going to say, but when it was his turn, he just put it out there: "I'm good at being a dad. I love being with my kids."

Molly was floored. She suddenly gave Roger a huge hug and said, "We don't have a lot of those around here."

Allison and another woman on our team started to talk with Molly. They found out that her father had left when she was young and that she had been raised by her mother and grandmother. Her grandmother had talked to her about God but died a few years later.

//Don't feel like you need to have a script, and don't be afraid to make mistakes.

"I've had no one to tell me about Him," Molly said. Allison shared how God is a good Father who would never leave her.

The two women exchanged contact information and began to meet together. Allison helped Molly grow in her relationship with God. But Roger, with his comment about being a dad, was the one who got to that deep place in her heart that caused her to open up. She saw a father's love, and she longed for it. That helped her be ready to hear the gospel.

As with anything else, spiritual conversations take practice to master. Don't feel like you need to have a script, and don't be afraid to make mistakes. Just start engaging in conversations. It may not feel natural at first, but push through. Over time, you'll get better at it.

Idols, Felt Needs, Lies, and Truth

When you're having spiritual conversations, there are a few things you want to look for. Ask God for discernment as you listen to what's on the heart of the people you're talking with. You can generally identify many of their beliefs, desires, problems, fears, perceptions, and thoughts in relation to these four categories.

- **Idols.** This word has some connotations that don't necessarily fit our culture today. You won't hear many people talk about bowing down to images. But that's not necessarily what this word is getting at. An idol is something people put their hope in that will ultimately fail them. Where are they placing their hope? What's shaping their identity? Is it a career, their health and fitness, a relationship, something material?

If those areas are where they are investing their hearts, they will eventually be crushed. All of that will let them down. As you identify idols, make a mental note of what they are, and when the time is right, gently challenge them. Point out that anything we use to define our identity or determine our hope other than God can be taken from us and will not satisfy our deepest needs.

- **Felt needs.** What are their felt needs? Are they lonely? Do they have broken relationships? Are they experiencing anxiety or depression? Did they or someone they love just receive a cancer diagnosis? We live in a broken world with broken people who need healing, reconciliation, and restoration. As you listen to people expressing what's on their hearts, these needs will come up. Many people who are struggling will be pretty honest with those they trust.

Your first response should be to acknowledge their struggle and empathize with it; then offer to pray for them. Prayer is powerful. When we pray, God moves. The key is that you actually pray! You can pray for them right there on the spot or on your own later. Even if they are not religious, offering to pray shows that you care about them. Eventually, you can point out that their pain matters because they are created by a God who loves them and that there is hope for healing because of Jesus's death and resurrection.

• **Lies.** What are they believing that is out of alignment with biblical truth? What false assumptions are obscuring their understanding of the gospel message? What lies do they believe about themselves, other people, and the world around them that need to be challenged?

There are many possibilities here: a belief that everyone is essentially good and that with the right public policies, laws, education, and environment and enough time, we can fix ourselves; a misunderstanding about sexuality and the purpose of sex and relationships; misperceptions about the church and morality. Listen with compassion, but also be prepared to point out the lies and offer a better perspective.

• **Truth.** Whether they realize it or not, most people already align with some biblical truths, like the student in the coffee shop who practically quoted Scripture without knowing it when trying to explain what it means to be human-centered. What do they already believe that you can affirm and use to build a bridge to the gospel? If you can identify ways they are living, character they are displaying, or things they believe that reflect biblical truth, it will give you opportunities to affirm and connect with them and eventually talk about what the Bible says.

There are many possibilities with this. For example, many secular people believe that all humans are valuable and deserve to be treated with dignity and respect, think love is the ultimate moral guide, or are passionate about caring for the marginalized and oppressed. These all align with the gospel and can be used as a bridge for introducing Jesus.

Affirming Truth, Challenging Lies

When you've identified idols, felt needs, lies, and truth, one area of conversation often leads to another. When you see a glimmer of truth in people, call it out. Tell them you respect or appreciate their view or their character. If they are gracious, kind, and generous, affirm them for it. Many Christians will look at qualities like that and think that if it's not coming from faith, it's not legitimate. But that's not the point. Something inside them identifies with truth, and pointing it out builds bridges. It creates a platform to talk about the gospel.

Identifying the truth in them gives you an opportunity to address their felt needs—to talk about hope for healing if they're in pain or hope for reconciliation if they have broken relationships. It's amazing how open people are to being prayed for once someone has seen who they are, validated their needs, and affirmed them for whatever in them is good.

When you've affirmed truth and addressed their felt needs, you can begin to challenge the lies and idols in their lives because it has become clear you're speaking out of concern. You can explain how those things are causing them harm and getting in the way of how God designed them. You've built credibility and trust to reorient their view of God: that He doesn't want to control them but rather longs to give them what's best for them.

Anti–Cancel Culture

In this era of "cancel culture," everyone is afraid to say something that will get them canceled—that is, blocked on social media. This has created an attitude of conformity and a fear of challenging mainstream narrative. Everyone is so careful to measure every word they say out of fear of offending someone. We've become much less open and honest and much more filtered because we're afraid of the consequences.

That's why it's so important to create an environment where it's okay to doubt and ask hard questions. You want to make it very clear that you will not be offended if someone disagrees with you, you aren't going to tweet about the conversation later, and they should not be afraid of accidentally saying something stupid, processing their thoughts in real time, or sharing incomplete ideas.

If you create an atmosphere of freedom, people will be drawn to it, especially if they are surrounded by toxic online interactions and have few people in their lives they trust.

That does not mean compromising your view of ultimate truth. There are absolutes, and you don't have to deny them. But most people, including you, haven't arrived at truth apart from some sort of process or journey of understanding. You have an opportunity to give people space for that—to create an environment they can pursue truth in without being judged for their thought processes and where debate and disagreement are healthy rather than threatening.

As you engage in spiritual conversations, remember that *you are not convincing them that you're right. You're encouraging them to pursue the truth*—ideally, together with you. There's a big difference between the two approaches.

In the first approach, you must have the answers. In the second, you don't have to pretend to know everything. You can be authentic and transparent. It's actually quite liberating. Jesus is the truth, so you can trust that an honest pursuit of truth will eventually lead to Him.

//You are not convincing them that you're right. You're encouraging them to pursue the truth.

This approach also levels the playing field. Rather than engaging with someone from a place of superiority, of having all the knowledge they are seeking, you engage them on equal terms. You're in this together. When you come with an "I'm right and you're wrong" attitude, it creates defensiveness. When you come with a "Let's do this together" attitude and exhibit some humility about it, they can open up to pursuing truth with you.

These discussions will raise many questions you may not know the answer to. People may have some perspectives that genuinely challenge you. That's okay. Be prepared to say, "I don't know," or, "Good point—I never thought of it that way before," or, "Let me look into that." It's actually very healthy and productive to explore the issue together and try to understand it.

This is not about having all the answers; it's about giving the Holy Spirit room to move as you discuss deep spiritual topics. And if He gives you some new understanding, too (a strong possibility), that's a good thing.

You'll often find that people's intellectual objections to the gospel are not the real issue. Underneath those objections is some kind of emotional wound or ongoing pain that is distorting their view of God, the Bible, the Church, or the gospel message. Deep pain frequently produces hostility toward the perceived source of pain that may not be based on any objective truth or logic.

That is where Spirit-led discernment comes in. Don't let the conversation turn into an argument. You don't want to win an argument but lose a friend. Be sensitive to not only people's felt needs but also their real, unexpressed, unidentified needs. Pray for their healing and restoration, and be patient. God knows the way into everyone's heart.

Have I Failed If I Don't Share the Gospel?

We've talked about spiritual conversations and gospel conversations, and it's important to understand the difference. Not every discussion will lead to the gospel message right away. It could get there eventually, although you may be just one person God uses as He pursues someone, and you might not see the end of the story. But even if you do, it can take time and multiple conversations.

Still, many people wonder if they've failed when a conversation does not lead to a presentation of the gospel message. And my answer to that is, "It depends."

As followers of Jesus who rely on the power of the Holy Spirit, we don't measure our success by results. Success is obedience. Did you do what God asked you to do? If so, that isn't a failure. For a believer, that's the definition of success.

Success comes from being in tune with the Holy Spirit and obedient to His leading. Sometimes He may urge you to prophetically call for repentance. Sometimes He may call you to simply be a friend. The key issue is whether you are really listening and obeying. Don't get down on yourself. There's grace and mercy and second chances—God is a master of all that!

//Success comes from being in tune with the Holy Spirit and obedient to His leading.

Paul wrote in 1 Corinthians 3:6, "I planted the seed, Apollos watered it, but God has been making it grow." Who was successful in that process? Everyone involved. Everyone has a role to play, but never forget the main character on the stage. You are not the hero. Jesus is. You can trust Him to work in the lives of those He is pursuing, even if you don't get to see the last act.

Often we celebrate only the moment someone makes a commitment to following Jesus—and, of course, we should celebrate that moment! Even the angels in heaven do (Luke 15:10). But we should also celebrate the moment when someone who was far from God takes one step closer to Jesus because they experience the sacrificial love from a Christian or because an intellectual or emotional barrier has been removed. Every step toward Jesus is a step that leads the person closer to making the most important decision of their life. It's a journey that usually takes time, so be patient.

A great example of this is Steiger's founding ministry, No Longer Music, a band that uses the stage to communicate the message of the Cross at nightclubs, festivals, and community gatherings to thousands of young people who might never step foot in a church.

If you want to learn more about how to use your creative gifts to share the gospel outside the Church, check out *Revolutionary! Ten Principles That Will Empower Christian Artists to Change the World*, by my dad, David Pierce. It is a powerful book that lays out biblically based principles illustrated by real-life examples for using one's art to change the world![15]

Call to Action!

• Pick a category from the list of spiritual topics mentioned in this chapter. Ask three non-religious people in your life the suggested questions. Draw out spiritual implications with follow-up questions. What stands out to you about their responses? Do you notice any idols, felt needs, lies, or truths?

• I encourage you to watch a few of the short videos from the IsThereMore? Spiritual Conversations series (available at Steiger.org). Pick one that you think would resonate with your non-religious friends. Share it with them and use it as a conversation starter.

• The Steiger team has developed *Steiger Streets*, a handbook for street evangelism (available at Steiger.org). Gather some friends and go to a place where young adults gather. Using the guide, spark spiritual conversations with young people. Start a group and join thousands of others around the world who are engaging our resources to reach the global youth culture in their city.

A Word from Chip to Parents, Grandparents, and Pastors

Before you move to the next chapter, stop for a minute and compare the approach that you just read with what we've typically said to reach our youth: "Come to church. This is what you need to believe. Here are the rules to keep. And try hard to be a good person."

I've sat in my living room with some people from the next generation who are in their early twenties. Some grew up in (well-meaning) homes and churches where they heard the above-mentioned messages. They got to college, their beliefs were challenged, and they shared for hours in our living room how they were currently deconstructing their faith, didn't know what they believed, and were totally confused.

We mostly listened, asked a lot of questions, and validated that it's okay to think, to doubt, and then invited them to explore as we built relationship around their spiritual issues, questions, and doubts. The response, after even a few weeks, was miraculous. The individuals weren't closed, they needed to be heard, and God worked in a powerful way.

You may not be ready to join Aaron and his team at the next gay-pride parade, but I want to share some very practical things that parents and grandparents can do to engage in spiritual conversations.

First, I want to encourage you to start where you're most comfortable. Maybe it's teaching your granddaughter some of your family recipes or taking your grandson on a hike. Let your spiritual conversations flow out of your shared interests and life lessons.

We don't always reap in the same season that we sow. Earning your children's and grandchildren's trust takes time. When they are confused and looking for advice, are you a safe person they turn to?

When the rubber meets the road, are you willing to set aside your religious and political boxes to be a missionary to the next generation? That might mean Grandma has to include her granddaughter's lesbian friend when cooking family recipes. By welcoming them into your kitchen, are you approving of their lifestyle?

Or are you going to sit by a well, like Jesus did, and break every taboo to share the gospel with the Samaritan woman?

Another great way to connect with your children and grandchildren is to share stories from your life, and not just the good ones. My grandson could relate to a time when I let my team down by missing crucial free throws and losing the game. My granddaughter leaned in when I shared about a devastating breakup and how it felt to be rejected. They began to see me as a real person with real problems.

Boldly take steps to move beyond concern and build bridges with your children and grandchildren. Keep the lines of communication open and strengthen the relationship.

4 // How to Introduce Jesus to Non-Religious People

Zara was raised in a strict Muslim family. But as she grew up, she adopted a "build your own" spirituality, an increasingly common choice in today's global youth culture.

For Zara, it was a mixture of Islam, Buddhism, and New Age ideology. She really was searching for truth, though. When she met a Steiger ministry team doing outreach on the streets, she was open to conversation.

One of the team members, Carolina, was bold with Zara: "I think Jesus wants you to know how much He loves you. He loves you so much that He died for you."

Zara had never heard this before. She asked how she could learn more about Jesus. Carolina introduced her to Diana, another team member. A few days later, the two women met for doughnuts and a spiritual discussion. Over the next few months, Diana and Zara stayed in touch, developing a friendship.

That friendship was a lifeline for Zara. When she broke up with her boyfriend, she shared about her depression and anxiety with Diana and asked for prayer. Diana prayed not only that Zara would find peace and comfort but also that she would feel the love of Jesus and know that He is God.

Zara was bursting with excitement when they met a few weeks later. She told Diana she had been experiencing an overwhelming feeling of love. She had a sense that God was personally revealing Himself to her.

Over the next two years, Diana and Zara's friendship took on elements of discipleship. They met on video calls to discuss the Bible and pray. Zara eventually realized she had found the truth she'd been so desperately searching for and asked Diana to lead her through a prayer of salvation so she could follow Jesus. She got connected with a church and invited friends who didn't know Christ to attend her baptism. Amazed by her transformation, many of those friends have continued going to church with her.

Zara went from a strict Muslim to a mix-and-match spiritualist to a sold-out follower of Jesus because someone had the boldness to befriend her and share the gospel with her.

Jumping Off the Cliff

My wife and I took our kids to the Black Hills of South Dakota a couple of years ago. We went to a spot where you could jump off a short cliff into a lake. My eight-year-old son stepped up to the edge. It was one of those moments of decision where you can't get any closer and the only thing left to do is either jump or bail out. Sometimes you just have to go for it. (He jumped.)

That's what introducing Jesus to someone can feel like. At some point, you've just got to do it. It may feel scary. You don't know how they'll react, and you probably won't say everything perfectly. That's okay. Fear doesn't disqualify you from being used by God; it simply reminds you of your dependence on Him.

//Fear doesn't disqualify you from being used by God; it simply reminds you of your dependence on Him.

If you've built a friendship with the person you're talking to and been able to have some spiritual conversations, take a risk. Where there's no risk, there's no faith, and where there's no faith, there's no power. Push through the fear and awkwardness. Recognize your "jump off the cliff" moments and take a step of faith by transitioning to a gospel conversation. You have the truth that heals, delivers, liberates, reconciles, and restores.

Expect Spiritual Opposition

There's nothing the enemy hates more than followers of Jesus sharing the gospel. Don't be afraid of him; Jesus promised we would overcome the power of the enemy and that nothing would harm us (Luke 10:19). But you should expect to be confronted with lies and discouragement.

The lies will generally aim at your identity and sufficiency. *Who do you think you are? You're a fraud, a hypocrite. You're completely inadequate. And why bother? They aren't going to listen anyway.* Thoughts like these may begin to flood your brain and make you think, *Maybe I'm not the right person for this.*

Every one of the common lies—those that question your identity, adequacy, and effectiveness—are easily and directly countered by biblical truth.

- *Your identity is in Christ.* You minister in His name, not your own.
- *You* are *insufficient,* but He is in you and is more than sufficient for every situation.
- *Your effectiveness depends on the Spirit, not your human effort.* Working within you, He is always able to accomplish His purposes.

The enemy's goal is to get your eyes focused on yourself and not God. Understanding who you are as a follower of Jesus empowered by His Spirit is the key to overcoming the lies.

Jesus is our example for standing on the truth when lies come. When He was tempted in the desert (Matthew 4:1–11), every response to the enemy's words was a quote from Scripture. Jesus stood on the Word of God to confront lies with truth. Like Him, we need to know biblical truth well enough to stand on it.

As we've discussed, sharing the gospel is not an individual sport. Don't do it alone. Commit to doing it with others so that when you're feeling weak, they can "hold your arms up" in battle (Exodus 17:10–13), and then you can support the others when *they're* feeling weak. The Christian life is meant to be lived in community with others.

And don't give up. If you're getting some spiritual opposition, you're probably doing something that matters. Constantly keep in front of you the importance of what you're doing, and remember that it's not about you.

Jesus and His offer of redemption are the only hope for this world, and He is deeply involved in the mission of getting that message out. God has opened your eyes to the world's sin problem, and He has given you the solution for it. He is walking with you and working through you as you build friendships with the non-religious and communicate the gospel to them.

The Person of Jesus

Remember, we aren't defending a concept, a philosophy, or a behavioral lifestyle. We're introducing people to the person of Jesus. The goal is not to convince people to believe a set of principles or a specific theology. It's to get them into a relationship with the living, resurrected Savior.

That should give you a lot of freedom. When you're engaging with a secular person, you don't need to focus on their behavior or any changes they'll need to make to follow Jesus. Their lifestyle and political views are not the main issue. Once they meet Jesus, all of that can begin to take shape. Your job is to facilitate that introduction.

The key issue in your gospel conversations is who Jesus is to them. What do they think of Him? Do they have an accurate understanding of Him? If not, you'll need to reframe Him for them.

The Real Jesus

To many nonbelievers, Christianity has become synonymous with certain political perspectives. In some secular circles, Christianity has also been unfairly associated with racism, misogyny, bigotry, and the exploitation of the weak by the rich and powerful. Many also point to horrible things done in the name of Christianity throughout history as proof of its destructive nature.

Jesus does not fit into the stereotypes people have of Him. As we're confronted by these misconceptions and misrepresentations of Jesus, we need to patiently let people know that we, too, reject the wrong perceptions of Him.

Jesus was radical. He subverted the cultural and political norms of His day. He was homeless, worked with uneducated working-class folks, spent time with the diseased and undesirables, defied boundaries between races and genders, healed the sick, and fed the hungry. Actually, many of the powerful and most religious people hated Him. That isn't the picture many people have of Jesus, but that's the picture we're given in the Bible. We can relate to Him.

//Jesus does not fit into the stereotypes people have of Him.

It's true that horrible things have been done in the name of Jesus. We should openly acknowledge that. But they aren't true reflections of who He is or what He taught. In fact, over the past two millennia, true Christianity has been a catalyst for amazing gospel-fueled societal revolutions. Christianity upended the destructive and distorted sexual ethics of the Romans; introduced the idea of orphanages, hospitals, and universities; fueled abolitionist movements; and much, much more.

The gospel has been astonishingly influential in shaping Western culture in positive ways. We need to reframe Jesus in the minds of our secular friends by placing Him in that context.

Bible Study for the Non-Religious

The best way to reframe Jesus is to go to the source: the Bible. Many secular people assume that they generally know what's in the Bible—as a moral guide, for example—but have never actually read it. One of the ways you can challenge misconceptions is by inviting people to participate in a Bible study with you.[16] Encourage them to find out for themselves what Jesus is all about. Just pick a book (any of the Gospels will work) and begin to read it together.

Make it clear that you aren't there to teach them but rather that you'd like to read with them and talk about what Scripture says. Maintain an environment where it's okay for people to ask questions and express doubts. It's fine if they say something that's a little "out there" or offensive. When you begin to expose people firsthand to who Jesus is, their understanding of Him will begin to shift toward the truth.

The Gospel and Your Own Heart

If you've grown up in church, sometimes foundational biblical truths can become overly familiar and mundane. We believe them, but they don't move our hearts anymore.

If that's you, ask God for a fresh revelation of the gospel. Jesus is the only hope for our world. Unless we truly believe that fact at our very core, our desire to share the good news will be weak.

As a young adult, I experienced a revelation of the gospel in such a profound way that it radically altered the trajectory of my life.

I grew up in a missionary home and have seen God's power at work. I feel very privileged that God was never just a nice Sunday tradition for our family. He has always been real to me. But my parents taught me that I needed to do whatever He called me to do, whether it resembled their ministry or not.

So, I went to college and studied international business and economics. At one point, I was also on my way to law school. I was very ambitious about changing the world through politics. Then I went on a church mission trip. I was reminded of the brokenness of the world—poverty, injustice, pain and suffering, young people like me who didn't have the privileges I had—and I remember having many strong feelings about it.

At first, I felt overwhelmed, as if anything I tried to do would be just a drop in the ocean. I wondered if there was any way I could have an impact. I remember complaining to God, struggling with Him for letting the world get messed up.

But then He gave me a fresh revelation of His truth. I realized that God is far from indifferent to our suffering. In fact, He sent Jesus—His only son—to enter into it. I realized that all the misery and pain in the world was due to just one thing: sin. And there's only one solution to sin: Jesus.

A Life-Altering Message

Those were truths that I had understood conceptually in my mind before, but suddenly, by the power of the Holy Spirit, they moved to my heart and exploded with life-altering significance. At that moment, I decided I was done with everything else in my life. I was going to address the root cause of the world's suffering and communicate its only hope: Jesus.

Don't misunderstand me. Followers of Jesus should be involved in every sphere of society. This is not an appeal for everyone to get out of business or politics or any other kind of work and commit to vocational ministry and missions. But all of us are called to minister to a broken world in whatever sector of society where we have influence.

Since that decision back in college, I've seen the transformational power of the gospel at work in the lives of thousands of people in almost every context imaginable: secular Europeans, Muslims in the Middle East, goths in Brazil, and so much more. I've seen people on their knees on city sidewalks to receive Jesus, people in hard-core nightclubs get a revelation of God, and people enslaved to sex or drugs or anything else be set free. Sometimes we forget how powerful the message of the Cross is, but it's what everyone needs to hear.

//Sometimes we forget how powerful the message of the Cross is.

That topic is where our spiritual conversations eventually need to go if God leads us into friendships that open people's hearts to it. Again, you haven't failed by not sharing the gospel if God uses you for only part of someone's journey toward Him. But a relationship with Jesus is His ultimate goal for everyone, and we can be completely confident of the transformation that relationship will bring to broken, hurting people.

Foolishness and the Power of God

Introducing someone to Jesus isn't just about helping them have a better impression of Jesus or see Him as a good teacher. Jesus is God Himself. What Jesus did for us on the cross with His death and resurrection is where we encounter God's power.

We're told in 1 Corinthians 1:18 that "the message of the cross is foolishness to those who are perishing, but to us who are being saved it is the power of God." This means that Jesus's death for our sins and His resurrection is both foolishness *and* the power of God.

There's tension between those two realities—on one hand, apparent foolishness, and on the other, God's power.

There are three key principles from 1 Corinthians 1:18 to keep in mind here.

• **This tension forces us to depend on the power of the Holy Spirit.** Depending on the Spirit is a good place to be. On the surface, our natural words come across as utter foolishness, but this message carries God's power and authority. We can't communicate it with clever rhetoric or brilliant reasoning. We need God's power. This means that we can't make the message of the Cross "cool." It's impossible to remove the foolishness. The only way it will "work" is if God moves supernaturally in the hearts of those hearing the message.

One of the signs you're filled with the Spirit is that you speak boldly. This was a sign throughout the book of Acts that those sharing their faith were being emboldened by God. There was power and authority in their words. We can still experience that today.

• We're reminded that sharing the gospel is not about our wisdom or eloquence.

Paul wrote that his message and preaching "were not with wise and persuasive words, but with a demonstration of the Spirit's power" (1 Corinthians 2:4). God's purpose is that when people place their faith in Jesus, it's based not on any human being's persuasiveness but on spiritual power. Their faith is birthed through Him.

I've often seen the importance of this. There are times when my words fall flat, and times when the very same words resonate because God's presence is in them. I know from experience that none of our natural efforts will bear spiritual fruit. We need to be praying for the Holy Spirit to give us boldness and courage so we can speak with conviction, assurance, and authority.

• People need to experience the power and presence of God.

This is what secular, post-Christian people desperately need. Many have intellectual problems with Christianity and the Church and don't just need another perspective; they need to experience God's power. That's why we have to communicate the good news of the gospel in such a way that we're fully dependent on God moving in their hearts and minds. If He doesn't show up, we've got nothing but foolish words. If He does, He powerfully convicts them of truth and reveals who He really is.

Especially in a post-Christian culture, where people think they know who Jesus is or have some idea of what the gospel message is about, experiencing God's actual presence and power makes all the difference. It breaks through the white noise of their religious assumptions and overcomes whatever hostility they've built up against the message. When God shows up in discernible ways, the conversation shifts from an intellectual matter to an encounter with Him.

The proclamation of the gospel needs to be accompanied by the power and presence of God. Sharing the gospel is not a transfer of information; it's a supernatural revelation of God Himself.

When we share the gospel itself, that kind of presence and revelation becomes part of the message. People sense God revealing Himself through our words. There's a sense of power and authority that goes beyond intellectual arguments, misconceptions, and biases. When we introduce people to the living God, He is there in the conversation.

The Power to Transform Lives

I've seen some of the most cynical, hardened people moved and transformed by the power of Jesus's resurrection. For a season, I served with Steiger's band, No Longer Music. We put on performances at public events to reach people who would never go to church.

At one of our events in Portugal, we were told as we were setting up that we would not be able to perform because of some problem with our permit. We prayed and asked God for wisdom, and I sensed Him prompting me to inquire if we could just do a short set. So I asked the officer if we could do thirty minutes, and she said that would be okay.

Our show usually takes an hour, and we had to cut it down without any time to plan or prepare. It was a rough and clunky performance, and I had a feeling it just wasn't connecting with the audience at all.

I was playing the main actor, who represented Jesus—we do a visual demonstration of the crucifixion and resurrection—and I was lying in a coffin, knowing I'd have to come out and preach to this crowd of secular young people. I felt as inadequate as I'd ever felt. Our half-hour show wasn't cool, I was sure it wasn't resonating with people, and I felt completely powerless.

I remember thinking as I lay there, *Lord, I don't know how I'm going to do this. But if You don't show up, this is going to look stupid. Please have mercy.* I jumped out and stood on stage, and the moment I opened my mouth, I felt God's authority almost like I never had before. His power was in my words. I'd experienced that in one-on-one conversations but not in front of a crowd. We invited people to respond, and the response was overwhelming.

After the concert, we had a chance to interview several different people about the show. They said some pretty amazing things:

> *In Belgium, we learn at school that God is not real. But you are very real about God. You really like Jesus, and it provokes me. It's just amazing.*

> *When I prayed with you two guys, I felt complete. I think it's the first time in my life I felt really complete.*

> *I'm going to believe in God. I'm going to find purpose in life, I think. Now I'm just living life day by day, but I don't like it. I just want a purpose to live for, a reason to live my life.*

> *After this kind of performance, I am able to say I can be a person who believes in God. In my heart, as a person who is a hard-core atheist, there is now a spark that has really started something big inside me.*

In human terms, we were putting on a show that was rough and ineffective and not going over well with the audience. Then the next moment, it dramatically unveiled truth and changed lives. What was the difference? It had begun to have the power and authority of the Holy Spirit in it. We took a risk of foolishness and experienced God's power. That power is available to everyone who believes. That's what we're depending on when we communicate the gospel message.

Your Words Matter

You've made a commitment to sharing the gospel, you've pressed through opposition, and you're ready to jump. Now what? Here are a few principles to keep in mind.

Rely on the Holy Spirit, not Scripts or Tracts

We live in a time when people are very skeptical of what someone is trying to sell them, and a script or tract feels like an attempt to make a sale. It's not relationally natural. People are much more open to conversations about things that matter to them, and sometimes those conversations go in unexpected directions. That's challenging when you're following a script. Just talk to people.

Remember that the goal is not for *you* to share the gospel; it's for *them* to hear and understand it.

Wait for the right opportunity. Be patient. Listen to the prompting of the Holy Spirit.

Avoid Using Christian Terminology

How do we communicate Jesus and the message of the Cross in language secular people can understand? We want to express truth in such a way that it's perceived as relevant. Or, to put it another way, we need to contextualize the gospel.

Contextualization is about communicating in a language people will understand. This goes back to understanding their inaccurate assumptions and recognizing when and how to challenge them so they can see who Jesus really is.

When we communicate in relevant, contextualized ways, we're better understood. To do that, avoid using Christian terms that sound foreign or strange to secular ears. Jesus contextualized His message for His audience, who knew a lot about agricultural and pastoral life in the fields. He described Himself as the Good Shepherd—an image that almost all His hearers could relate to. He described the Kingdom in terms of catching fish and spoke of seeds being sown into the ground and growing up to bear good fruit. He used words and images that were relevant to them.

//Contextualization is about communicating in a language people will understand.

But if I go into a major U.S. city and start illustrating the gospel with images of shepherds and fishermen, something is going to be lost in translation. People would generally understand, but the message wouldn't really resonate with them. That's why contextualizing is important. Language can be powerful, and it needs to connect with people's hearts.

Contextualizing the Gospel

The best way to contextualize the gospel is to connect each element to an idol, felt need, lie, or truth that we identify in our spiritual conversations. Here are the core truths of the good news and how they connect to our spiritual conversations:

• God created us to be with Him. *(This is the basis for all human value, purpose, morality, identity, and relationships.)*

• Our sin separated us from a holy God. *(This is the cause of all pain, suffering, and evil in the world.)*

• We cannot fix ourselves. *(No good deed, political system, book, philosopher, or self-help guru will solve our sin problem.)*

• Jesus, God's Son, entered into our world as a man, lived a sinless life, performed countless miracles, died on the cross to pay the punishment for our sins, and rose from the dead three days later to defeat death. *(Jesus's work on the cross is the only solution to our sin problem.)*

• Everyone who trusts in Christ alone will be reconciled and have eternal life. *(Jesus's redemptive work is our source of forgiveness, acceptance, and hope for the future.)*

• The Holy Spirit empowers us to live life with Jesus today. *(When we make Jesus lord of our life, the Holy Spirit gives us supernatural love, joy, peace, identity, and purpose that cannot be shaken.)*

Don't Use the Bible as Proof

The Bible is the authoritative, infallible, and inerrant word of God. But when I'm having a spiritual conversation with a secular person, they don't believe that. It may be interesting to them, but it isn't seen as authoritative.

Many young people today consider the Bible to be, at best, a collection of ancient myths that can be a moral guide for some, but not universal or something to be taken literally. Others actually see the Bible as a dangerous work of fiction that is extremely outdated in its treatment of slavery, homosexuality, and morals. Sadly, most have never actually read the Bible for themselves.

Clearly, we should never compromise the message or downplay the authority of the Bible in our conversations, but we also can't use the Bible as argumentative proof. "The Bible says X, therefore Y is true" is not a compelling or effective approach for post-Christian people.

Instead, we need to leverage the fact that the Bible is experientially verifiable. By that, I mean that we need to show the Bible is true because it offers the most rational and compelling explanation of our reality and deepest longings.

For example, most people will admit that there is something transcendent about the love of a parent for their children. It's hard to believe that a mother's love for her baby is no more than a chemical reaction in the brain that evolved over time to ensure the survival of our species. When I look at my son or daughter, do I really believe that they are just an evolved biological organism with no more worth than a plant or a dog? No! Even the most nihilistic atheist would have a hard time believing that.

The Bible tells us that God knew us before we were even born (Jeremiah 1:5), knit us together in our mother's womb (Psalm 139:13), created us for a unique purpose (Ephesians 2:10), and loved us so much that He sacrificed Himself for our sake (John 3:16). In this context, the truth of Scripture speaks powerfully to a non-religious person because it has been connected to their lived experience and longings.

So, while we don't want to totally dispense with the Bible in our conversations, we do need to take a different approach in how we share biblical truth. We can't prove that something is true "because the Bible says so" when we're talking with someone who doesn't accept Scripture as true, but we can tie their experiences and feelings to what the Bible says and how it points us to eternal life, meaning, and purpose.

Bring Up the "Unknown God"

The apostle Paul was brilliant at adapting the way he communicated the gospel to his audience. In Acts 13, for example, he drew heavily from Scripture when he was speaking in synagogues and in front of Jews and God-fearing Gentiles. But in Acts 17:16–34, when he spoke in Athens to sophisticated pagan philosophers, he never referred to Scripture at all. He knew his audience.

Paul's message in Acts 17 is a great example of how to communicate the gospel in a post-Christian culture. When Paul arrived in Athens, he spent some time observing and listening in order to truly understand the culture. Then Greek leaders brought him to the Areopagus to present his ideas to leading philosophers.

First, he complimented the Athenians on their interest in the gods (verse 22). He noticed what was good and affirmed the truth he saw in them. Like many people today, the Athenians had a desire to understand truth and were open to the idea of supernatural, invisible realities. That's worth affirming.

Paul then referenced an altar he had seen there that was dedicated to an "unknown god" (verse 23). Greek pagans were aware that they might be missing someone in the Pantheon, so they kept a monument to whichever deity that was, and Paul quoted one of their poets (verse 28), much like someone today might quote the lyrics of a pop song and connect them with a deeper truth.

Paul even summarized the biblical account of Creation without ever referencing Genesis. But he still presented the truth, even though it contradicted the Athenians' understanding and assumptions. Then Paul took a step of faith and "jumped off the cliff" by calling his audience to repentance and preaching the death and resurrection of Jesus (verses 30–31). He didn't actually mention Jesus's name, but it was clearly understood whom he was talking about.

Those Spirit-empowered words were not well received by everyone and did not make Paul popular (a few believed, but many didn't), but they did make people more curious, and many wanted to know more (verses 32–34).

That's a perfect example of contextualizing the gospel for a specific audience. It gives us a biblical basis for adapting our approach without compromising the message, depending on the worldview of the people we're talking to and the context of our conversations. It's a great model to follow.

There's Power in Your Story

One of the most powerful things you can share is your own story. Outside of a courtroom, *testimony* can come across as a very religious word, and we tend to share our testimonies in very religious ways. But the language of those stories can be adapted and communicated in a variety of contexts. And your own experience, which no one with a relativistic mindset can deny (and generally won't if you've become friends and established credibility), can carry a lot of weight.

//One of the most powerful things you can share is your own story.

If you've been having spiritual conversations with someone, the idea of sharing your experiences may have already come up. If you've listened to other people's stories, they will eventually ask you about *your* story and what you believe. As Peter implied, people may ask you to explain "the hope that you have" (1 Peter 3:15), especially if they see it in the context of some hardship or adversity you're going through. If you aren't prepared to answer, and to do it in a way that doesn't sound churchy or hyper-religious, sharing your testimony is probably going to feel uncomfortable.

This is something you can practice. Think of how you came to believe in Jesus and follow Him and how that has made a difference in your life. Figure out how to express that without using religious language, and then get the story down to around three to five minutes. Be sure to include the gospel message. Write it down (not so you can memorize the script but so it will eventually begin to feel natural to you) and practice reciting it with a friend or family member. When the time comes, you can draw on that preparation and share your testimony in a way that feels and sounds natural.

Take a Risk and Invite a Response

Many people get all the way up to sharing about Jesus and fall short by not inviting a response. It feels risky, maybe as if it will forever sour the relationship (which it probably won't), and becomes a huge hurdle that someone just can't clear. But we have to give people an opportunity to say yes or no to Jesus.

Anyone in sales will tell you how important it is to give people the chance to say yes or no. Again, we aren't salespeople—we're building actual, genuine friendships as expressions of God's heart toward those He loves—but Jesus does call people to make a decision about Him. And although we don't use sales techniques, we can learn some things from salespeople about the dynamics of decision-making. At some point, and maybe several times, we need to give people the chance to say yes to Him.

If they say no, it doesn't mean the end of the friendship—not if you've established a sense of connection and trust and have created an environment where it's okay to question, doubt, and process thoughts out loud. But they might actually say yes. I've been in situations in which presenting the choice to them seemed kind of like a last resort and my expectations were low, but it can be surprising and amazing when God moves someone to believe in Him. It's another one of those cliff-jumping moments that feels risky but is incredibly worth it when God shows up.

Discipleship Relationships

When we have the boldness to step outside the church walls and share our faith, we find that some people are open and ready to hear the gospel. But then what?

There's a huge gap between church culture and secular culture. Many people are interested in Jesus but not at all in the Church. The pathway between encountering Jesus and walking into a church is much longer than it used to be.

Walking with people like that in a discipleship relationship is critically important. In order to see long-term fruit, we need to share our lives deeply and sacrificially with those who have been reached. Paul expressed this in his first letter to the Thessalonians: "Because we loved you so much, we were delighted to share with you not only the gospel of God but our lives as well" (2:8). Like God, we invest in those we love and pursue.

A discipleship relationship doesn't start the day someone commits to a local church; it begins when they meet a follower of Jesus. That's when Jesus's discipleship relationships began, isn't it? People met Him and then followed Him, and He began speaking truth to them from day one.

This is not a program. Rather, it's about walking alongside people. The act of sharing the gospel may happen in a classroom or a church building sometimes, but it doesn't have to. It can happen in the environment people come from, right where they are. In fact, one of the ways we raise up disciples who make disciples is by teaching them how to be followers of Jesus in their own context.

Discipleship should always lead to multiplication. We disciple people so they can disciple others who in turn disciple even more people. Part of walking with Jesus is bringing other people into a relationship with Him. That's what leverages your ministry. You don't have to worry about reaching everyone. You may have two or three discipleship relationships, but they can each have two or three of their own, and the impact keeps multiplying exponentially.

Once discipleship becomes a lifestyle, you'll find it very satisfying and maybe even addictive. You'll see the potential fruitfulness of building relationships with a few people who build relationships with others. It's liberating to stop viewing the issue of reaching our culture as an overwhelming impossibility and instead focus only on the people God has put in front of you. One step at a time, as you pursue those He leads you to, build relationships with them, open up spiritual conversations that eventually lead to gospel conversations and an opportunity to say yes to Jesus, and walk with them in discipleship relationships, your world will begin to change.

Call to Action!

Paul exhorts us in 2 Timothy 4:2 to "be prepared in season and out of season" to preach God's Word. Opportunities to share Jesus will come at both expected and unexpected times. The key is to be ready when the moment arrives. Take these steps to be prepared:

- Write out your personal story and the gospel (separately and combined) using your own words. (Note: This is not a script to memorize but rather a framework for sharing your story and the gospel message.)
    - Make it short and succinct (under five minutes).
    - Don't use religious language.
    - Include a clear invitation to respond.
- Practice sharing the gospel and your story with a friend in a conversational way.

- Ask God to give you the chance to tell your story.
- Commit to walking with those who want to learn more or make a decision for Christ.
- Host a Bible study for the non-religious in your home, in a café, or even remotely.

A Word from Chip to Parents, Grandparents, and Pastors

If after reading this chapter you think, *I can't imagine the youth in our church [or my son/daughter or one of my grandchildren who are very far from God right now] coming back to Jesus,* then let me provide some wonderful hope.

Theresa and I have opened our home to the next generation. We've built friendships, started spiritual conversations, led Bible studies, and had a front row seat to God's work in these young people's lives. God is speaking to them, and they are responding by exploring His Word with new eyes.

In fact, I want you to pause and imagine the joy, after faithfully praying and building a relationship with your child or grandchild, in receiving the ultimate answer to prayer: They make a public declaration of their faith in Christ. You're so relieved that you think, *Oh good, now everything is okay!* Instead, we should see their new life in Christ like a newborn baby who needs the right care, feeding, and nurturing to grow up into a healthy adult. New believers need to be discipled.

Discipleship can be an intimidating word, especially for parents and grandparents. We have to remember that discipleship takes time; there aren't any quick fixes. We spare no expense to ensure that our children get the best coaching, training, and tutoring to be on the traveling team or become a great musician or get into the best undergraduate program. But how seriously are we taking their spiritual and moral development?

Are we outsourcing it to the Church, Christian school, Bible camp, or youth group? Are we living out our faith through one-on-one conversations, modeling what we learn in Deuteronomy 6:7, which says, "Impress them on your children. Talk about them when you sit at home and when you walk along the road, when you lie down and when you get up"?

The research is unmistakable: The most powerful influence on our children is what they see in their parents' lives. Are we living out our faith?

Let's be intentional about building into the minds and hearts of our children and grandchildren, whatever age they're at and stage of life they're in, to help them grow in the knowledge of God, walk with Him, and begin to discover His purpose for their lives.

5// Navigating Politics, Sexuality, Science, and Other Divisive Subjects

In May 2020, Minneapolis was the center of the political universe in the aftermath of the George Floyd killing. Walking with our local outreach team near the place where Floyd died, I saw buildings still on fire from the rioting the night before. I stood overwhelmed by the brokenness of this world, watching a huge crowd of mostly young people. They were crying out for justice.

It struck me that they were looking for human answers to social problems that were actually spiritual problems. I turned to Cyrena, a team member who is African American, and said, "Hey, why don't you go up there and ask for the microphone?"

Cyrena is very bold. She just went and asked, and they handed the mic to her! She began by singing a song, which drew people in. Then she shared how the ultimate solution to the brokenness of the world is Jesus. People were glued to her message. She invited people to receive Jesus, and many prayed out loud on the spot.[17] *Our team then spread out to listen, pray, and engage with people in spiritual conversations. I have rarely experienced people more receptive to the gospel than the young people of Minneapolis were that summer.*

The Opportunities of Hot-Button Topics

Topics like politics, justice, sexuality, and science can be very divisive. In our increasingly secularized culture, it can be intimidating to speak into these issues. It often seems like we have to choose between silence and a debate. But rather than avoiding these subjects or getting angry, we need to realize that these matters are incredible opportunities to engage in spiritual conversations. They can open up all kinds of discussions about the real root of life's problems. To do so, we need to reframe our perspective so that we approach the topics not in a combative way but as opportunities to begin conversations that set the foundation for sharing the message of Jesus and the Cross.

//We need to realize that these matters are incredible opportunities to engage in spiritual conversations.

Winning the Heart, Not the Argument

The following framework is simple and practical. It addresses our attitude as well as our approach: what we say and how we say it. Both elements are important and go together.

First, we tackle tough subjects with humility and compassion. When we engage people about these topics—or really any topic—we should reflect the heart of Jesus with an attitude of radical love, humility, patience, and compassion. Our goal is always to win the heart, not the argument.

Second, we need to remember not to make secondary things primary. It's easy to get caught up in trying to change someone's political or moral views, but those are downstream issues—something for the Holy Spirit to address further into an individual's discipleship journey. Our primary goal is to introduce the person to Christ.

Think of it like a double-sided funnel with Jesus in the middle. On the left side are the topics and issues that need to be addressed to open people's hearts and minds to Jesus. These are the lies, idols, misconceptions, hurts, and confusion that obscure people's views of Jesus. Then on the right side, there are things like moral behavior, political ideology, and non-salvific theological doctrines that should be addressed after someone puts their trust in Jesus. If we focus on issues on the right side of the funnel before the person has met Jesus, then we are putting the cart before the horse. It's not to say that morality, politics, and other secondary issues are not important; it's just that they need to be addressed in the proper order.

Affirm, Reframe, and Challenge

Third, as you engage in these challenging topics, you should follow this process: *affirm*, *reframe*, and then *challenge*.

It is important to affirm whatever is true or admirable about someone or their viewpoint. It might be hard to see, but some commendable motive or sentiment is usually there. Then we reframe the opposing argument, pointing out underlying false assumptions. Finally, we gently challenge the untruths that stand in the way of the Cross.

That framework—beginning with a heart of humility and compassion, remaining focused on the primary issue of introducing someone to

Jesus, and affirming the individual, reframing the argument, and challenging false assumptions—is a powerful way to navigate those difficult discussions. Let's look at how it applies in each situation.

Politics

Discussions about politics have ruined more than a few Thanksgiving family gatherings. We live in a hyperpolarized society that is divided concerning issues of politics and social justice. Differing political views are often at the root of strained or broken family relationships, yet few topics offer more natural opportunities to spark spiritual conversations.

Keep in mind that the purpose of this section is to equip you to reach non-religious people who would not walk into a church today. It is *not* to make political statements or address how Christians should or should not engage the political process. The whole point here is to show how political conversations can become spiritual ones that lead to Jesus and the Cross.

Fear and the Political Savior

Much of the Christian response to the decline of Christian influence and to the moral decay of society has been characterized by fear. Every year, new books are published that foretell the inevitable downfall of American society. Podcasts and blog articles decry the evil forces at work to undermine godly values and marginalize Christian voices. As this hostility against believers continues, it is not hard to imagine a day in the near future when pastors could be handcuffed and incarcerated for preaching biblical truth or when Christians could lose their jobs for not affirming the secular ideology of our day.

But all of this rhetoric, even if it's true (and there are reasons to believe it is), has only created a culture of fear and hostility in believers. Of all people, followers of Jesus should be known for hope, not fear. We have a hope that cannot be shaken by circumstances, precisely because we do not put our faith in earthly things. We are not called to place our hope in a political party or leader or even in the constitutional religious freedoms our country has given us. Our hope is in Jesus alone. I am not advocating for political apathy or for abstaining from the political process. As Christians, we should seek to engage and influence every sphere of society.

Even if our country collapses and Christians are persecuted, as in the first-century Roman Empire, we still have hope because we know we are "foreigners and exiles" (1 Peter 2:11) on earth and that "our citizenship is in heaven" (Philippians 3:20). Our well-being is based firmly on a God who takes care of us, not on political systems and movements.

Fear is insidious. It clouds our thinking and causes us to react defensively. Fear makes us see secular people as enemies, which causes us to adopt a zero-sum-game mentality of winning and losing. And if the very survival of Christianity is at stake, the goal of saving our country from "the enemy" justifies any means of achieving that goal, even if those means are completely anti-Christian in attitude and approach.

Sadly, this fear has led many Christians to look at political power as a savior, as though political solutions or politicians will preserve and restore godly values to our society. Of course, this is similar to what people in Jesus's day were looking for: a political solution to the oppression of Rome. Their search for a political answer caused them to miss what God was doing. It was the antithesis of Jesus's mission on earth.

So, each of us needs to ask ourselves, *Am I hope driven or fear driven?*

Us Versus Them

In political discourse, it's easy to fall into the tribal "us versus them" mentality, even if "them" is just an exaggerated caricature that bears little resemblance to the complex, nuanced reality. We construct oversimplified, cartoonish straw men and talk about "them" without actually having thoughtful conversations with real people who think differently than we do. That makes it really easy to dislike or even hate people on the "other side." "They" become the enemy rather than human beings who bear God's image.

I once became friends on Facebook with a pastor I respected. I appreciated his biblical teachings but didn't realize until we were Facebook friends how politically outspoken he was. There's nothing necessarily wrong with expressing strong political opinions on social media, but his approach and tone surprised me. I could tell from the way he talked about "them" that he did not have any Facebook friends who saw things differently—or if he did, they unfriended him a long time ago. All he did was shout into his social media echo chamber filled with like-minded followers. He had zero influence on anyone who didn't already agree with him, all while fostering a culture of fear and hostility toward "them."

How do you talk about people who are politically opposed to you? Do you envision real people with hopes and fears, just like you? Do you see them as people Jesus loved so much that He died on the cross for them? Or do you view them as people with malicious intentions who are out to demoralize our culture? Are they to be loved and pursued, or feared and avoided?

We need to remember who the real enemy is. It's true that we're in a war, but it's not a war against other human beings. It's against "the spiritual forces of evil in the heavenly realms" (Ephesians 6:12). It's a war for (not against) the souls of a generation who have been deceived.

It's much better—and much more biblical—to err on the side of love than on the side of defensiveness. If I assume the worst in people's intentions and motivations, it does not help me foster a love for them. Consider Jesus's example in Matthew 9:36: "When I saw the crowds, I was *angry and defensive* because they were *malicious and plotting* to hurt me" (emphasis added).

Jesus's reaction makes sense, right? It's only natural to be angry and defensive toward people who are out to get us. But, of course, that is not what Matthew 9:36 actually tells us. Rather, it says, "When [Jesus] saw the crowds, he had *compassion* on them because they were *confused* and helpless, like sheep without a shepherd" (NLT, emphasis added).

//Fear and hostility make us want to put our fists up, ready for a fight, whereas, the compassion of Jesus makes us stretch out our hands in love.

Compassion should be our attitude toward people we disagree with. Fear and hostility make us want to put our fists up, ready for a fight, whereas the compassion of Jesus makes us stretch out our hands in love.

Love Your Enemy

During one of our outreaches in the aftermath of the George Floyd tragedy, I met a young woman who described herself as a revolutionary Marxist. *Wow,* I thought. *In the minds of my conservative friends, this woman is the enemy personified.*

I asked her what she thought would be the solution to our social problems. She spoke very passionately about upending our political institutions and systems of oppression. She believed society needed to be reeducated. Politically and ideologically, I was opposed to her, but I admired her passion. She recognized the brokenness of the world, her heart was broken for people who were abused and oppressed, and she wanted to do something about it. Her worldview was wrong, but in many ways her heart was right.

If you can see people with a heart of compassion and consider their underlying assumptions, you soon realize that often their motivation is technically "good." They are simply operating under a different worldview. They want to fix the problems of this world, and they believe they are doing the right thing. So rather than choosing malice, I choose to believe that people have just not met Jesus yet.

Making Secondary Things Primary

The next step is to remember our focus. Some Christians seem more passionate about their political affiliation than about Jesus. They focus more on fighting downstream battles like abortion and freedom than on introducing people to Jesus. They get stuck in secondary battles and forget the primary goal.

Don't get me wrong: Laws and policies are important for establishing justice and truth in society. We do need to engage in the political process and bring our values into it. But when we focus on laws alone, we're like a doctor who only treats symptoms but never deals with the root disease. Laws and policies don't get to the cause of society's problems, which are, at a very fundamental level, about sin and brokenness.

Our primary goal as believers is always to reach secular people and bring them into a relationship with Jesus. And to do that, we need to get the conversation out of the political box and avoid fruitless debates about secondary or symptomatic issues.

A Passion for Justice

This post-Christian generation is passionate about fighting injustice, and this creates a great opportunity for us. This activist spirit comes out of a God-given desire within all of us to use our lives to make a difference in the world. Because it's based on making wrong things right, it operates on a framework that ultimately connects to the gospel.

A video promo featuring the singer Billie Eilish captures this generation's sense of activism perfectly. It begins with shots of young people on their phones and echoes the complaint of older generations that today's youth are always attached to their screens: "obsessed, disconnected, not in the moment." Then the promo goes on to show all the ways they are using their phones for creative purposes, social causes, and advocating for change. The video ends with a provocative question: "So maybe next time they see us staring at a screen and they ask us what we're doing *on* it, why don't we show them what we're doing *with* it?"[18]

This generation's desire to right the wrongs of the world is expressed in several cultural hot topics:

- Environmentalism
- Racism
- Sexuality and LGBTQ+ issues
- Feminism
- Mental health and suicide prevention
- Economic injustice

Those are the issues this culture cares about, and even though their positions on the issues can become twisted or even anti-biblical, the motivation behind them might not be.

Reframing Justice

To reframe justice, then, we would affirm these desires and point out that we were all created for truth, justice, and good works. Even if young people don't believe in God, He has put it in them to live not just for themselves and pursuing pleasure and happiness but also for more transcendent values and truths. That's commendable.

We looked earlier at the opportunities we have in our spiritual conversations to find the truth in the beliefs of non-religious people and then affirm it. Here are some points of connection with biblical truth we can use to do that:

- Political and social activists believe the world is not as it ought to be.
- They want to be part of something bigger than themselves.
- They care about the marginalized and the oppressed.
- They believe in justice, which is based on a moral code.

Once we affirm the heart behind political activism and express that we're on the same page in some ways (as we also have the desire to do something to address society's problems), we can begin to identify lies and idols:

- The secular worldview says that there is no outside, transcendent authority that defines our identity, morality and purpose. (A lie.)
- The secular worldview believes that with the right laws, education, and time, we can fix ourselves. (A lie.)
- Many people are putting their hope in a politician or political system that will ultimately disappoint and fail them. (An idol.)

From there, we can raise spiritual questions that begin to challenge whether the problems really have political solutions or if there's something deeper at work. Here are a few examples:

- Why is the world so broken? Why is corruption and oppression so universal?
- Given enough time, can a person, a culture, or even a country solve all its problems? Why or why not?
- I believe that love is the ultimate moral ethic. Do you agree? What is love? Where does it come from?
- Are there things that are right or wrong for all of us, regardless of popularity or opinion? If so, where does that come from? Who decides?
- If we are the result of an evolutionary process of the survival of the fittest, why should I deny myself for the sake of others? Why should I care for the weak, oppressed, or voiceless?
- Do you believe in universal human rights? Isn't it a colonial imposition for us in the West to impose our view of human rights on other cultures? Or is there a moral code that transcends all cultures? If so, where does it come from?

Finally, we can transition from a spiritual conversation to a gospel conversation:

- Christians point to God as their external standard. By measuring themselves against Him, they can arbitrate among human opinions. What do you make of this? What's the alternative?
- I believe that Jesus came to our world and sacrificed Himself to fix a problem (sin) we couldn't fix ourselves. Have you considered if this is true?

By following this process, you can learn to see political issues like these not as conversations to avoid but as ways to connect, approaching people with humility and a genuine desire to seek those answers together.

Challenging Assumptions

I saw a group of tough-looking young men during an outreach at a lake in Minneapolis. They had tattoos all over their bodies. I went up and started talking to the guys.

"What do your tattoos mean?" I asked one of them. Tattoos are personal and often visible, so they're an easy topic to connect on.

"Which one?" he asked.

"Well, how about that one?" I pointed to a circle with three arrows pointing diagonally to the bottom left.

He explained that the arrows represented anti-fascism, anti-capitalism, and anti-authoritarianism.

"Oh, okay," I said. "Why do you believe in those things?"

He talked about corruption of the system and how the wealthy were oppressing the poor, how billionaires were living on their yachts while ordinary people suffered. He was passionate about socialism as the means to bringing equality to society.

A well-meaning Christian man who had joined us on the outreach began to argue for capitalism as a better system (a fair political point, but not at all the purpose of the conversation). It was not a time to get into a debate about capitalism versus socialism; I was trying to make a connection. So I kindly but firmly took back control of the conversation and followed the "affirm, reframe, and then challenge" process.

I affirmed this tattooed anti-fascist by telling him that I respected his concern about pain and suffering and his willingness to do something about it. I agreed that the world is broken. "I'm an activist too," I explained. "A Jesus activist."

Then I reframed. "But the problem is that no matter what political or economic system we put in place, we can't seem to rid ourselves of evil and suffering. I believe that's because the core problem is corruption of the heart, and no political system can solve it." I used words like *corruption* and *system* because they were part of the young man's language.

Finally, I challenged. I told him that as a follower of Jesus, I believed we can't fix ourselves—that the only solution is spiritual renewal and restoration that comes through the death and resurrection of Jesus.

We had a long and productive conversation. The anti-facist eventually opened up and said he had attended a funeral the day before. A pastor there had talked to him about God too.

"I think God is pursuing you," I told him.

He looked at me and said, "Yeah, I think you're right."

For some Christians, a heavily tattooed left-wing political activist might appear as "the enemy." If we're only interested in making political points, our response might be to stand against him. But we have a much higher goal. And we can realize the goal surprisingly often if we affirm, reframe, and lovingly challenge.

Sexuality

Sexuality is undoubtedly the issue that draws the most hostility from secular people toward the Church. If you're going to engage secular culture, questions about LGBTQ+ issues are going to come up. They are unavoidable.

Society's attitudes toward LGBTQ+ issues have changed rapidly in recent years. The number of people who identify as LGBTQ+ is growing dramatically with each generation. According to Gallup, 20.8 percent of Gen Z in 2021 identified as LGBTQ+—nearly double the number of millennials and much more than older generations.[19] As more and more people identify themselves outside of traditional gender categories, more and more people consider these identities normal and acceptable. They have become mainstream.

There is very little room in today's culture for reasonable conversations that challenge that narrative. Discussions about LGBTQ+ rights are emotionally charged and draw on themes of justice and equality historically connected with the civil rights movement of the 1950s and '60s. Secular workplaces celebrate pride month with no regard for those who don't agree with it. LGBTQ+ allies can be vicious in their defense. Anything less than total affirmation of all things LGBTQ+ is quickly labeled as homophobic and bigoted.

For Christians who hold to a traditional, biblical sexual ethic, the thought of engaging in these conversations can be paralyzing.[20] So how should a faithful follower of Jesus live in a "pride month" kind of world?

Love Is Love?

The first step in engaging this topic is to recognize that beneath the mask of intense moral conviction, there is deep confusion and brokenness. This very circular statement illustrates it: "Love is love."

This banner statement for LGBTQ+ rights implies that people should be free to love whomever they want however they want and that all loves are equal. Our culture is very confused about love. Messages about it on social media and in pop culture oscillate incoherently between the hedonistic unshackled lust of hookup culture and the deep desire for a "you complete me" soulmate level of intimacy with "the one."

//Human beings are desperate for belonging and acceptance but have no idea where to find them.

The reality is that we can get caught up in the confusion. Human beings are desperate for belonging and acceptance but have no idea where to find them. Even within the LGBTQ+ movement itself, there's a lot of division and incoherence.

Lesbians and old-school feminists are fighting over the transgender movement because, after all, what are women's rights if there's no such thing as a woman? Mental healthcare is in disarray, no longer seeking to align people's mental state to their physical realities or objective truth but instead looking to align their bodies to their psychological feelings. This is a very disorienting time.

Jesus's response to the confusion of His day was compassion. As we saw earlier, He looked with compassion on the crowds who were "confused and helpless, like sheep without a shepherd" (Matthew 9:36, NLT). *Compassion* means to "suffer with," so empathy is the key. As we reach out to the LGBTQ+ community and their allies, we need to start from a place of radical love and mercy, like Jesus did.

Understanding Same-Sex Attraction

If we're going to engage the LGBTQ+ community with compassion, we need to better understand the realities its members live daily. It's true that much of the explosive growth in those who identify as LGBTQ+ is social contagion or a fashionable trend, as it has become more accepted and even celebrated in society. But many people really do experience same-sex attraction, gender dysphoria, or other sexual and gender-related abnormalities.

This may include you. If you are a Christian who is experiencing any of this, I encourage you not to hide it. Find a Bible-believing pastor or friend you trust and share your feelings with them. The enemy wants nothing more than for you to struggle alone in shame and condemnation.

Debates have raged over the years about whether people are born gay or choose homosexuality. The truth is that reasons for homosexuality are complex and diverse. They aren't the same for everyone. But generally there are three essential reasons people experience same-sex attraction or gender dysphoria, and someone might experience it for any of these reasons or some combination of them, possibly all three.

- *External sin:* the sin others have committed against people, such as sexual abuse or being an absentee father.
- *Personal sin:* the sin people may have committed themselves, such as viewing hard-core pornography or being sexually promiscuous.
- *Fallen nature:* the consequence of the fall in Genesis 3. Our bodies are broken and imperfect through no specific fault or sin of our own or others. We may experience impulses that are not in line with God's original design for our bodies.

In John 9, Jesus and His disciples met a man who had been blind since birth, and the disciples asked who had sinned: this man or his parents. The disciples assumed that his blindness was the direct result of external or personal sin. Jesus replied, "Neither this man nor his parents sinned," and then redirected the whole question away from causes and into purposes: "This happened so that the works of God might be displayed in him" (verse 3). The passage tells us that the man's physical disability was not the result of personal or external sin and also that God will redeem our broken bodies for His glory.

This means that experiencing same-sex attraction is not un-Christian any more than it is un-Christian to get sick. These are physiological issues. Knowing that helps us understand and empathize with people who are dealing with physical impulses that the majority of us don't have to deal with.

Temptation Versus Sin

It's important to make a clear distinction between temptation and sinful action. Temptation itself is not a sin. An action (whether in thought or deed) that results from temptation is sin. One is a blameless universal experience; the other is a bad choice.

We know there is a firm distinction between temptation and sin because Scripture tells us that Jesus was "tempted in every way, just as we are—yet he did not sin" (Hebrews 4:15). That means that experiencing same-sex attraction is not a sin, but to act on that temptation (in thought or deed) is.

We are to some degree the product of the sin of others, our own sin, and our fallen nature. This is the human condition. That's why we must approach this topic with humility, empathy, and compassion.

Empathy Versus Agreement

As we saw in chapter 2, one of the lies of our culture is that in order to love someone, we must affirm their lifestyle and behavior. This is one of the biggest obstacles we face in our approach to issues of sexuality. If we want to engage with secular people on the topic of

---

//We can disprove the false equivalency of love and agreement by actively loving people we disagree with.

sexuality, especially if there is hostility involved, we need to deal with the question of whether love equals agreement.

The reason this is so challenging is that sexuality has been tied to identity. A rejection of someone's sexuality is therefore seen as a rejection of their core essence, their entire understanding of who they are. Words are not going to change that, so the best way to challenge this lie is with action. We can disprove the false equivalency of love and agreement (that to love someone implies affirming their lifestyle) by actively loving people we disagree with.

Simple Demonstrations of Love

We were once doing an outreach when two young gay men walked by. We had some free water and I asked if they wanted some. They said yes, and as we were all talking together, they asked what we were doing there.

"Oh, we're Christians," I said, "and we just want to serve and talk to people."

"We're not religious," one of them said.

"That's fine," I told them. After we talked for a little while and they made it clear they were a couple, I asked, "What's going on in your life? Is there anything we can pray for?"

As it turns out, the mother of one of them had cancer. I asked if we could pray for her, and the man said that would be okay. I put my hand on his shoulder and prayed for healing and for God to give them peace and show them His love.

When I finished, one of the guys looked at me and said, "Man, I'm not religious, but that was really cool."

That example is a simple way to demonstrate love. It's not a statement of affirmation for a lifestyle; it's an expression of someone's value as a human being and how God loves them.

During another outreach, Cyrena and I met a guy named Josiah in a park and started up a conversation with him. We asked what was going on in his life. He had just recently moved to Minneapolis and didn't know many people there. He told us how he grew up in a Roman Catholic family but walked away from Catholicism while he was in college. He came out as gay and recently had broken up with his boyfriend and was feeling pretty lonely.

We'd been clear up front that we were Christians, but he was comfortable talking about his personal pain. We asked him many other things, too—people are more than their sexuality and have a lot more to talk about—and he told us he was an artist and showed us pictures of what he had been creating.

I told him I had a bit of a business background and said I might have some ideas that would help with his business plan for his art. A few weeks later, we met at a coffee shop, looked over his business plan, and talked about some things that would help him run his business well. Then I began to challenge him gently.

"Being in business is hard," I said. "In order to survive the inevitable storms and disappointments, you need to find something to hold on to—an anchor that can't be shaken. I know that no matter what I do or what happens to me, God's love will never change. He is my anchor. That's where I find my identity, as a beloved child of God. So, what will be your anchor in the storms?"

I continued, "Once you've found your anchor, you need to find a higher purpose. Making as much money as possible isn't a big enough goal. It will not sustain you." I went on to share my belief that we were each put on this planet for a purpose and are called to find what that purpose is and live it out.

Do you see how the flow of the conversation worked? It was a friendship conversation with a post-Christian guy who had grown up in a church and was walking in a lifestyle that might have caused him to see Christians as his enemies. We spoke openly about God, but our talk in the coffee shop that morning never got into an explicit gospel conversation. It did address some false assumptions about the relationship between love and affirmation (I demonstrated genuine love without agreeing with his lifestyle), and I was able to lovingly challenge his stated identity and self-described purpose, often the two stumbling blocks for people in the LGBTQ+ community.

Those are the kinds of conversations we need to engage in if we're going to reach the LGBTQ+ community. The discussions have to be real, honest, and compassionate, all of which build trust, break down stereotypes, and demonstrate God's heart.

Challenge: Purpose

From an apologetic perspective, the key assumption in the sexuality conversation is the concept of purpose. Is there a transcendent universal purpose for sex, marriage, and our bodies? Or are marriage and traditional sexual ethics a social construct that can or should be abolished for the sake of personal happiness?

// A person's sense of purpose shapes everything about them.

If sex is simply about the pursuit of pleasure and fulfilling natural instincts and desires, you'll approach it as a personal choice, and that choice may shift over time. But if sex has an ultimate purpose and design, that changes things, doesn't it? That's why my conversation with Josiah went in the direction it did. A person's sense of purpose shapes everything about them, including what they do with their body.

In the secular world, meaning and purpose are self-defined. There is no transcendent designer who has imparted a particular way to live our lives. There may be a vague spirituality and a concept of God, but not one that requires personal accountability, at least in the area of sexuality. In this worldview, sex—now devoid of the consequence of procreation, thanks to contraception and abortion—is a personal source of pleasure and self-expression governed only by the concept of mutual consent. That's the sole moral principle involved.

I heard a quote in a conversation that sums up the sexual ethics of secular culture: "You can't be your whole self if you listen to the rules of others." If that is the case, sex is about self-actualization, freely expressing yourself, becoming whole.

Sadly, the consequence of this sexual free-for-all tells a different story. Loneliness, anxiety, and depression are at epidemic levels, especially

advent prayer

Gracious God, you are the giver of all that is good. I come with open hands to receive your grace-filled gifts.

I give you my hurt and receive your hope.
I give you my worry and receive your peace.
I give you my grief and receive your joy.
I give you my fear and receive your love.
I give you my life and receive your Son.
Jesus. Savior. Lord.
I praise you. I worship you. I love you.
Now and always.
Amen.

date night

February 2 | 6:00-8:00 pm

You're invited to a free event at our Chanhassen campus featuring Jason Earls — comedian, pastor, and father of six. Jason and his wife Terri will be sharing stories of the joy and humor in parenting.

Event details and registration:
westwoodcc.org

among young adults. Sexual violence has been linked to the copious amounts of time devoted to viewing increasingly hard-core pornography. Today's sexual ethics have led not to freedom and fulfillment but to bondage and addiction.

On the other hand, in a Christian worldview, we were created intentionally by God. His design for sex, marriage, and our bodies is not about control or limiting our happiness but about protecting us from harm and allowing us to thrive spiritually, emotionally, physically, and sexually. In contrast to the predominant sexual ethic of our day, God's way leads to genuine freedom and fulfillment.

When a secular person asks for my view on sexuality, I say, "I would love to share, but if you really want to understand my view on sexuality, you need to hear about it in context."

Then I explain how I believe that every human being has infinite value *because* we were created by God. This God is not an angry judge but rather a good father. He knows us, loves us, and created us for a purpose, and because of that, every person, without exception, deserves to be treated with love, dignity, and respect.

This challenges the narrative that to disagree with people implies hate or phobia or some other form of rejection. I'm insisting on their value in God's eyes and their rights as human beings, something that the secular worldview has no basis for.

Then I say, "Because we were created by God for a purpose and He designed us to live a certain way for our own good, His rules have nothing to do with control or limiting our freedom. Like a good father, He wants the best for us, and when we align ourselves with His design, we thrive. So I believe that God designed sex to be shared between one man and one woman in the context of marriage and that this is for our good."

Now, they may still strongly disagree with this perspective, but at least I've been able to *reframe* a positive vision for biblical sexuality and *challenge* the narrative that Christians are hateful and homophobic.

Meet Jesus

People in the LGBTQ+ community and the global youth culture in general, especially those who grew up as part of a church, have a very legalistic view of Christianity. They believe that to become a Christian means having to first change their lifestyle and behavior—that they have to act and live a certain way before they will be accepted, which isn't true at all. They don't understand God's grace and unconditional love.

Submitting our sexuality to God's design is a discipleship issue based on trust that God is good and that His ways are better than ours. Until someone has an encounter with the living God made possible by Jesus's death and resurrection, surrenders their life to Him, and invites the Holy Spirit to dwell in them, none of that will make any sense. Giving up their sexual identity seems impossible until they know that God is good and trustworthy.

That's why the highest goal must always be to lead them into an encounter with Jesus, not to convince them to adopt our moral framework. He is the ultimate answer to finding the intimacy everyone seeks. He's the only one who will satisfy our deepest desire for belonging and acceptance.

When we experience the profound love of Jesus and understand the beauty of who He is and what He has done for us, everything the world has to offer pales in comparison. Like an old hymn says,

> Turn your eyes upon Jesus,
> Look full in His wonderful face,
> And the things of earth will grow strangely dim
> In the light of His glory and grace.[21]

So, rather than focusing on people's sexual behavior, we need to focus on introducing them to the person of Jesus. When someone meets Him, experiences His overwhelming love for them, and surrenders their life to Him, surrendering their sexuality to Him actually makes sense because they have a new identity in Christ. In committing to following Jesus, they are convicted and empowered by the Holy Spirit to make Him Lord of every part of their life, including their sexuality.

Science

"I can't take Christianity seriously. It completely contradicts science."

These were the words of Jackson, a young man with a bodybuilder physique wearing a rainbow-colored tank top whom I met during an outreach in Minneapolis. He is a health freak but also really into psychedelic drugs. He told me he grew up in a Catholic home but is an atheist today. He rejected his religious upbringing because he believed it was incompatible with science and rational thought.

"I can't believe the Bible," he continued. "It says the world is only ten thousand years old."

"Well, no. The Bible does not actually say that the world is ten thousand years old," I replied.

I explained that the biblical account of Creation in Genesis does not describe the specific scientific process of how the world came to be. Rather, the intent of Genesis 1 is to show that the universe, and everything in it, was created by God, on purpose. It is not the product of random chance.

On top of that, according to the Bible, every human was made in the "image of God" (Genesis 1:27), which gives us special value and purpose distinct from animals. Our worth and ultimate satisfaction is found in a personal and loving relationship with our Creator.

After that exchange, Jackson and I became friends. Even though we have very different views of the world, I really like him. He is intelligent and thoughtful but not at all arrogant. We've spent hours at his hipster loft in Minneapolis engaged in intense conversations about all kinds of questions related to science, the Bible, and life.

How Science and Faith Fit Together

Many secular people today like Jackson assume that science and religious beliefs are entirely incompatible. That's interesting because even though secular people are receptive to spirituality, most still have a naturalistic perspective, where everything must have a scientific explanation.

They hold these contradictions by separating science and spirituality into two boxes: science as the realm of facts, and spirituality as the realm of subjective feelings. And yes, ironically, that is in reverse when it comes to gender: Feelings are facts, and science (biology) is subjective. (Remember when I said that this is a confused culture?)

The assumption is that religious belief is mainly a matter of faith and feelings, while the secular worldview is mainly based on reason and logic and that you can have reason or faith but they don't overlap.

//The assumption is that religious belief is mainly a matter of faith and feelings, while the secular worldview is mainly based on reason and logic.

In our spiritual conversations with our non-religious friends, we need to challenge the assumption that the Christian worldview is based solely on (blind) faith and that the secular worldview is based on reason.

Actually, the secular worldview is built on faith just as much as the Christian worldview is. We cannot definitively prove there is a supernatural, transcendent reality, but we also can't prove that there is none. So, when secular people demand unquestionable proof of Christians, they are demanding something that they cannot give for *their* view either. In fact, some of the secular worldview's most strongly held beliefs (particularly regarding justice and equality) are based on highly questionable assumptions.

Think about it: How can we reconcile the belief that the human race is the result of an evolutionary process of the survival of the fittest and yet believe in human rights, equality, and individual freedom? To believe in these things as a non-religious person requires tremendous faith.

Plausible and Desirable

As we challenge the false "faith" assumption, our goal is to open our non-religious friends' minds and hearts to sincerely and honestly considering the God of the Bible. Many people have dismissed Christianity as a viable option because they believe it to be implausible (rationally) and undesirable (emotionally or morally).

Those are two barriers that need to be overcome for someone to contemplate the truth of the Bible and seek God sincerely. In order to get people to seek the truth honestly, we must do the following:

- Máke it plausible (mind).
- Make it desirable (heart).

Plausibility comes by us offering various forms of evidence that shows that the Christian worldview is rational and a reasonable explanation for the world as we know it.

//This challenges the assumption that to be a Christian, I have to throw my brain in the trash and just have blind faith.

In a skeptical world, we need to be prepared to share why we believe what we believe. Some reasons are emotional or experiential, and that is perfectly acceptable. But there are also many reasons that are rational and based on a variety of objective scientific, moral, historical, and philosophical evidence.

The goal is not necessarily to get someone to admit that you are right but rather to show that it's perfectly reasonable for an open-minded person to consider all the angles and come to the conclusion that the

Christian worldview is the best possible explanation for our world. This challenges the assumption that to be a Christian, you have to throw your brain in the trash and have blind faith.

Desirability comes from contrasting the implications of the two worldviews. The Christian worldview provides hope for eternal life, an intimate relationship with a loving God, and a logical basis for human value, justice, and equality, whereas in the secular worldview, there is no transcendent purpose. It offers nothing but blind indifference to our personal suffering and pain, and all that we experience while alive is entirely meaningless and will be quickly forgotten.

By showing that Christianity is both plausible and desirable, you open people's hearts and minds to honestly considering whether the God of the Bible is real. Some people may never have honestly thought about it. But now they may be willing to read the Bible for the very first time.

As the Holy Spirit softens their hearts, they may sincerely and earnestly seek whether God really is there and whether the claims about Jesus might actually be true.

God promises in Jeremiah 29:13 that if you "seek [Him] with all your heart," you will find Him. God is actively pursuing His people. If our non-religious friends seek Him openly, earnestly, and sincerely, they will encounter the living God in a way that science cannot explain.

Apologetic About Apologetics

You don't have to be an expert in apologetics or well versed in the ontological or cosmological arguments for the existence of God in order to challenge the notion that believing in Him is completely irrational. As you develop friendships and engage in spiritual conversations with people, you will inevitably encounter tough questions and objections that you will not know the answer to, and that's totally okay. Be prepared to say, "I don't know," and "Let me look into that," or, better yet, "Let's look into that together."

It goes back to the idea that we are not trying to convince people that we are right; rather, we're encouraging them to pursue the truth.

When you encounter specific challenges (e.g., the reliability of the Bible, supposed endorsement of slavery and genocide in the Bible, the problem of evil or suffering, the hypocrisy of Christians, corruption or abuse within the Church, or the doctrine of hell), don't be intimidated; instead, see the challenges as opportunities to learn.

Ask God for understanding in prayer, search Scripture for answers, read thought-provoking books, and seek the counsel of wise Christians. There are good answers to these tough questions. As you dig into them and learn, not only will you be able to answer the questions but it will strengthen your own walk with Jesus as well.

Recommended Reading on Apologetics

- *The Case for Christ* (Lee Strobel)
- *Evidence That Demands a Verdict* (Josh McDowell)
- *I Don't Have Enough Faith to Be an Atheist* (Norman L. Geisler and Frank Turek)
- *Making Sense of God* (Timothy Keller)
- *The Reason for God* (Timothy Keller)
- *Return of the God Hypothesis* (Stephen C. Meyer)

Genesis and Evolution

One of the major stumbling blocks for secular people when considering Christianity is the apparent contradiction between modern science and some of the events described in the Bible.

On one hand, this is because secular people have no category for the supernatural, so when they see something miraculous or supernatural in the Bible, they assume it is a mythological or "god of the gaps" explanation (the idea that humans have always attributed to God phenomena that have not yet been explained scientifically). The assumption is that there is always a natural explanation for supernatural events.

On the other hand, it's because Christians have at times unnecessarily interpreted biblical texts as specific scientific explanations for how something came about. The biblical account of Creation in Genesis 1 is a prime example.

In order to interpret Scripture accurately, we need to understand the cultural context and the author's intent. It's important that we don't look for answers to questions that a particular passage in the Bible is not trying to answer.

Let me be clear: I believe that the Bible is the only infallible, authoritative Word of God. The Bible is without error and 100 percent true in all that it intends to communicate. In Genesis 1, for example, the author is not trying to provide a scientific explanation of the creation process. The author is writing to affirm that God did, in fact, make the world but not to explain the details of *how* He made it.

So, although Genesis 1 is limited in its scope, it does not cease to be the Word of God. The biblical account neither affirms nor denies the specific scientific theory explaining the creation of the universe, other than that it was clearly not the result of blind chance.

There are two definitive truths we can draw from Genesis 1:

- All things were created by God with intentionality and specific purpose.
- Humans have unique value and purpose among creation because we were created in the "image of God" (verse 27).

But are we undermining the authority of the Bible by not taking it literally? No. A key to solid biblical interpretation is understanding its literary genre. Much of the Bible is written in a poetic genre that draws on analogies and metaphors, while other parts are historical accounts meant to be interpreted literally.

The book of Psalms, for example, is read as poetry, whereas the Gospel of Luke and the book of Acts (an eyewitness account written by Luke) are read as history, including the accounts of miracles.

The challenge is that in some parts of the Bible, the genre is not as easily identifiable. This is certainly true for Genesis 1, which has led sincere Bible-believing Christians to different conclusions. Some have interpreted the chapter as a literal six days (the "calendar day" view), others as a series of geological ages (the "day age" view), and still others as a literary analogy without any sequential connection.

There will always be debates about how to interpret some passages, including Genesis 1. But it is incorrect to argue that if one part of

Scripture can't be taken literally, then none of it can be. That isn't true of any human communication.

In the end, our personal interpretation of the creation account is not a central theological tenet necessary for salvation. So when we are engaging non-religious people with the gospel, we should not confuse or distract them by focusing on our particular view on Creation or other secondary theological issues.

Rather, we should focus on Jesus and the message of the Cross and, in the case of Genesis 1, the gospel truth that God created all things intentionally and with purpose.

Only after someone understands and accepts that the God of the universe entered into our world as a man born of a virgin, lived a sinless life, performed countless miracles, died on the cross to pay the punishment for our sins, and rose from the dead three days later to offer new life and reconciliation to all mankind should we consider engaging the various secondary questions about creation, evolution, and other non-salvific topics.

The Courage to Act

Hebrews 11:6 says, "Without faith it is impossible to please God, because anyone who comes to him must believe that he exists and that he rewards those who earnestly seek him." The part that says "anyone who comes to him must believe that he exists" seems obvious. But what does it mean to truly believe that?

Let me illustrate it this way. My dad tells the story of a group of English soccer fans who were in town and decided they wanted to fight with a gang of Dutch drug dealers. Our family's apartment overlooked the main drug-trafficking street, and my parents watched as about eighty people gathered, armed with bricks, bottles, and clubs. Soon, screams and the sound of breaking glass reverberated as the battle began to rage.

Suddenly a solitary police car screeched into the parking lot across from our building. An officer jumped out of the car and ran into the angry mob, baton in hand. Then something surprising happened. Although the mob could have eaten this guy for lunch, they dropped their makeshift weapons and fled, with the lone officer holding the rubber stick in hot pursuit.

Then in a moment of lucidity, the police officer realized what he was doing and raced back to his police car. But for a few crazy moments, that cop had believed that the power and the authority of the law was greater than that of the unruly mob.

That is what believing that God exists looks like. Believing He exists means that I am so convinced of the authority and power of the One I represent that I would run into the middle of a riot for His sake. It is in the riots—those moments when we have lost the illusion of control and depend entirely on God—that we experience His supernatural power.

The apostle Paul says in 1 Corinthians 4:20, "The kingdom of God is not a matter of talk but of power." If you want to experience God's transformational power at work in the lives of people all around you, you need to act. You can't wait for everything to be perfect or for all the circumstances to align. You just have to take a step of faith.

No Risk, No Faith, No Power

To do this requires courage. Courage is not the absence of fear but rather a willingness to do the right thing despite the fear you feel. It has been said that courage is the ability to do something that frightens you.

//If you want to see God move in your life, you'll have to step through fear and take risks.

Everyone faces fear. It's normal to be afraid. Even the great apostle Paul said, "I came to you in weakness with great fear and trembling" (1 Corinthians 2:3). That is good news because it means that if you are afraid, you are in no way disqualified to be used by God.

If you want to see Him move in your life as you navigate discussions about politics, sexuality, science, or any other divisive subjects with your secular neighbors, you'll have to step through fear and take risks, for where there is no risk, there is no faith. Where there is no faith, there is no power.

Where do we get that courage? We find an answer in Acts 4:13:

> When they saw the courage of Peter and John and realized that they were unschooled, ordinary men, they were astonished and they took note that these men had been with Jesus.

The reason that Peter and John had courage was not that they were smarter or more skilled than others; it was that they had an intimate relationship with Jesus. The closer you are to Him, the more intimate you become with Him, the bigger He becomes to you, and the smaller the world's obstacles become in comparison.

Courage grows over time. It is like a muscle: The more you use it, the more it grows. Courage is more about one thousand small decisions than about the one large one. It's a lifestyle of saying yes to God.

A Word from Chip to Parents, Grandparents, and Pastors

I know what some of you are probably thinking: *Wow, this book was really pretty good until it got to this chapter. Has Chip gone woke? Doesn't he understand the dire straits that we are in, what's happening to our country, and the need to do whatever it takes to "make America great again"?*

Yes, I understand, and no, I haven't gone woke, but my question to you would be this: Has our approach to addressing the issue to "make America great again" been done in such a way that it has made the gospel, the truth of Scripture, and biblical morality secondary to our national/tribal agenda?

Our country is divided, families are divided, and churches are divided over blue- and red-state issues. How did politics in America become more important than the Great Commandment, the Great Commission, and our relationships with our families and brothers and sisters in Christ?

Is there a vital role for politics? Absolutely. Do we need to be Christian citizens, run for office, vote for those who hold biblical values, lead in our communities by joining the board of education, and winsomely take a stand for truth exercising our constitutional rights? Absolutely!

But do Christians, in the name of saving America, call people names, diminish others, label people, and treat others without dignity? Do they put aside the character flaws and lack of biblical morality of certain leaders as long as they champion results that we believe are important? Are we willing to mortgage the gospel at all costs and alienate the next generation who see the hypocrisy and wonder how people (often parents, grandparents, and pastors) who claim to be followers of Jesus could treat others so harshly and see those who believe differently as "the enemy" instead of considering them lost and in need of a Savior?

Do I believe in America, am I patriotic, do I believe we need to make some drastic changes in our country? Of course! My father fought in Iwo Jima, got a Purple Heart, and lost countless friends to preserve our freedom. The question is, how do we go about it?

When I scroll through social media and see the vitriol of self-professed Christians toward those who disagree with them, it breaks my heart. The scorn is pushing the next generation away from God.

Are you willing to rethink what really matters? Are you willing to put aside these very important but *secondary* issues so that the gospel, eternal life, and the truth of Jesus in Scripture can be heard by the next generation?

Are you willing to take the suggestions in this chapter to heart?

Jesus modeled how to stand for truth, love His enemies, and overcome evil with good. The Roman Empire and its evils, injustice, and disregard for followers of Jesus was transformed by radical followers who lived out their faith, forgave their enemies, treated everyone with respect, and worked with such excellence that they found themselves in positions of great influence.

The younger generation is not beyond reach, but those of us who are older must build the bridges that allow them to see the real Jesus, understand the real gospel, and be part of God's solution for the world.

We can do nothing less!

conclusion

God is up to something.

Recently, I spoke to a room full of passionate Christian leaders in their early twenties in Minneapolis. I was sharing about the global youth culture, the seductive lies of secular humanism, and the devastating impact it's having on young people all over the world. I explained that in Jesus's death and resurrection, we have the ultimate hope the world is looking for but, sadly, many are not looking to the Church for answers.

I told them that like what happened with Nehemiah, our hearts should break for this generation because a broken heart will compel us to action. I then reminded them that a broken heart starts with repentance.

As I was speaking, I noticed a young man crying. I looked across the room, and it was clear that the Holy Spirit was moving, so I cut off the rest of my talk and just invited everyone to respond.

Soon, these young men and women were all on their knees, praying prayers of repentance, crying out in anguish for their lost friends, and asking God to send them to boldly proclaim the truth to their generation.

I want you to know that despite all the reports of decline of Christianity in our country, there is hope. God is not done with us yet. He is raising up people, young and old, to bring the truth of the gospel to a generation that is confused and helpless.

And God wants to use you, too.

My prayer is that this book has been a source of hope and encouragement for you. I pray that as you put the principles into practice, God will use you to bring the life-changing message of Jesus to people who are far from Him.

notes

1. Ryan P. Burge, "Gen Z and Religion in 2022," *Religion in Public* (blog), April 3, 2023, https://religioninpublic.blog/2023/04/03/gen-z-and-religion-in-2022.

2. Burge, "Gen Z."

3. Burge, "Gen Z."

4. Unsigned TikTok video, transcription shortened and adapted, from "eve_wasframed," January 31, 2022, www.tiktok.com/@eve_was-framed/video/7059426902154726702.

5. Lydia Saad, "U.S. Confidence in Organized Religion at Low Point," Gallup, July 12, 2012, https://news.gallup.com/poll/155690/confidence-organized-religion-low-point.aspx.

6. Jeffrey M. Jones, "Confidence in U.S. Institutions Down; Average at New Low," Gallup, July 5, 2022, https://news.gallup.com/poll/394283/confidence-institutions-down-average-new-low.aspx.

7. To watch a video that gives a fuller description of global youth culture, visit www.youtube.com/watch?v=6Tl_PlWbJEA&t=4s.

8. "Almost Half of Practicing Christian Millennials Say Evangelism Is Wrong," Barna, February 5, 2019, www.barna.com/research/millennials-oppose-evangelism.

9. Lady Gaga, Goodreads, https://www.goodreads.com/quotes/288926-don-t-you-ever-let-a-soul-in-the-world-tell.

10. Richard Weissbourd, quoted in Emily Boudreau, "Combatting an Epidemic of Loneliness," Harvard Graduate School of Education, February 9, 2021, https://www.gse.harvard.edu/news/21/02/combatting-epidemic-loneliness.

11. Allison Davis, quoted in "Dating Games," *Land of the Giants* (podcast), January 11, 2023.
12. Peyton Cardoza, "Honey and Glass," 2020.
13. Dale Carnegie, *How to Win Friends and Influence People* (New York: Gallery Books, 2022); originally published by Simon and Schuster in 1936.
14. Timothy Keller, posted on Twitter by @timkellernyc, March 12, 2022.
15. Side note for creatives: Are you an artist, musician, singer, designer, filmmaker, or any other kind of creative? Art is a powerful tool for communication truth. The principles of spiritual conversations can be applied to any art form. A piece of art has the unique ability to draw you in (friendship), challenge your perspective (spiritual), and proclaim the truth (gospel), all in one piece, movie, performance, or song.
16. Go to Steiger.org to check out free resources for Bible studies to use with the non-religious.
17. Watch a video of Cyrena's powerful preaching that day at https://vimeo.com/steigerint/cyrena.
18. Billie Eilish, "What We Do Next," Deutsche Telekom advertisement, https://vimeo.com/448462712.
19. Jeffrey M. Jones, "LGBT Identification in U.S. Ticks Up to 7.1%," Gallup, February 7, 2022, https://news.gallup.com/poll/389792/lgbt-identification-ticks-up.aspx.
20. For more information, visit https://steiger.org/sexualityresources.
21. Helen H. Lemmel, "Turn Your Eyes upon Jesus," public domain.